Powerful Spaces

On the Studio series

Today, well-founded training is a high priority in the architectural profession. Often, talented architects teach at universities, thereby communicating their charisma and enjoyment of teaching while training the next generation of architects. In doing so, they fulfil an important general social and cultural teaching task.

This volume introduces a new series of books from Quart entitled Studio. The title refers to students, their studies and teaching, which today mainly takes place in studios, i.e. small, intensively guided learning groups.

The teaching often focuses on an architectural theme that is aimed at ultimately leading students to specific design questions. That theme also forms the guiding principle of the individual volumes in the series, connecting the various chapters, including underlying texts by the teaching architects, lectures, presentations by guest authors, students' designs and finally the presentation of exemplary buildings by the architects.

Further volumes will follow, allowing the series to grow into a review of contemporary architectural teaching in Switzerland. The book series provides a forum for teaching architecture and is aimed at inspiring discourse.

Heinz Wirz

Studio No.1 **Powerful Spaces** **EPFL**
 Giuliani Hönger **2013 – 2015**

Quart Publishers Lucerne

Imprint

Giuliani Hönger. Powerful Spaces
Volume 1 of the series Studio

Edited by	Heinz Wirz, Lucerne
Concept	Heinz Wirz
	Giuliani Hönger, Zurich
Project management	Quart Verlag, Linus Wirz
Articles by	Christian Hönger and Lorenzo Giuliani
	Tibor Pataky
	Joseph Schwartz
	Raphael Dunant
	Michael Meier
Editorial	Heinz Wirz
Foreword	Andrea Bassi, Geneva
Translation	Benjamin Liebelt, Berlin (G–E)
	Monique Dorang, Berlin (F–E, Foreword)
Graphic design	ATLAS Studio, Zurich
Lithography	Printeria, Lucerne
Printing	DZA Druckerei zu Altenburg GmbH

© Copyright 2016
Quart Verlag Luzern, Heinz Wirz
All rights reserved
ISBN 978-3-03761-149-4

Also published in German:
ISBN 978-3-03761-135-7

Quart Verlag GmbH
Denkmalstrasse 2, CH-6006 Luzern
books@quart.ch, www.quart.ch

Une beauté forte	Andrea Bassi	7
Powerful Spaces	Lorenzo Giuliani, Christian Hönger	9
On a spatial category in the work of Giuliani Hönger and the design studio Powerful Spaces	Tibor Pataky	27
Load-bearing structure and spatial formation On the cooperation between architects and engineers	Joseph Schwartz	37
The design studio Powerful Spaces, Student Projects, EPFL, 2013–2015	Raphael Dunant, Michael Meier	45
Four built spaces	Lorenzo Giuliani, Christian Hönger	65

Une beauté forte

Swiss architecture largely owes its international reputation to the quality of its structures, and it is this concrete aspect that harbours its poetic strength. Here, architecture is not reduced to a mere structural concern. Rather, regardless of the theoretical approach adopted, architecture maintains a relation between the conceptual intention and the real object, a sort of invisible cement which allows the beholder to perceive its beauty. This beauty may express itself through varying degrees of intensity; it may be elegant, unassuming or distinct and may also be qualified by other fitting terms.

During the two years of project work at the École Polytechnique Fédérale de Lausanne, Lorenzo Giuliani and Christian Hönger laid down the theoretical foundations of their *recherche patiente*. While subscribing to the structural orientation foreseen by the project laboratory, they clearly engaged in a collaboration with students which focused on the intimate relationship between space and structure.

Their attitude, the perseverance in research, and the openness and culture crucial to this exploration yielded remarkable projects. The pertinence of observation became manifest in a dialogue evolving between the student project and the proposed theoretical framework, thereby bringing to light the pedagogical and didactic quality of the project assignments. The fine relation between the works of Giuliani Hönger and the transfer of knowledge to a future generation of architects added further depth to their theoretical training.

The beauty perceived in the relationship between space and structure is evident and closely related to the nature of the structure itself. It is a beauty which becomes distinct by virtue of the accuracy of structural intentions.

Andrea Bassi
Professor EPFL 2007–2015

Powerful Spaces

Lorenzo Giuliani, Christian Hönger

We both developed a special interest in space independently of each other during our studies. From that perspective it may not be a coincidence that we both subsequently became Assistants to Professor Ernst Studer. He had developed stimulating light studies on the Pantheon[1] in Rome and constructed an impressive interior with the church in Sarnen 1964–1966.[2] Both spaces inspired us to reflect and influenced us. Many years later, on a joint visit to one of our completed buildings, an architectural photographer surprised us with the statement that several of our projects are characterised by a yearning for powerful spaces, which moved us both. The diagnosis of our passionate search for powerful spaces may well be fitting, but we ourselves were by no means so clearly aware of this yearning—and of the fact that it is noticeable in a number of spaces we have built.

What does "powerful space" mean?

In every period, an attempt is made to find a final definition of architecture: be it the search for the right or contemporary style, the ideal fulfilment of functional requirements, an *architecture parlante* or the question whether architecture is art.

The insight that architecture should be regarded not only as one of the above aspects, but primarily as the discipline of space and spatial design—on all levels from the city to the interior—was supported during our years of study in the 1980s at the ETH Zurich. In the following years of our own office activities, we became aware that as allrounders, we must know the basics of many related professional fields in order to design in an integral way. In daily work, the architectural elements that are the means of forming architectural space are focused upon in discussion. However, our actual aim and focus of interest lies in emptiness itself. In stating that, we are aware of the paradox of Martin Heidegger that the quality of the emptiness of space is defined by the surfaces of its boundaries.[3] Our work has confirmed to us that the core field of architecture is the question of space, because it is the only field in which we can claim to be specialists.

1 Ernst Studer / Daniel Studer, "Licht und Schatten im Pantheon", in *Archithese* No. 1, 1997, p. 25–33.
2 See the essay by Friedrich Achleitner: "Extreme, Mode, Tabus", in Thomas Boga / Ernst Studer: *Werkstattbericht 1, Ernst Studer Architekt. Ausstellung an der ETH Zürich vom 21. April bis 12. Mai 1977*.
3 Martin Heidegger: "A space is something enclosed and released, namely within a boundary [...]. The boundary is not something where something finishes, but instead, as the Greeks recognised, the boundary is where the nature of something begins. [...] The nature of space is the enclosed, set in its boundaries," [trans.] in id., *Vorträge und Aufsätze. Bauen Wohnen Denken*. Stuttgart 1997, p. 149.

Ernst und Daniel Studer, Licht und Schatten im Pantheon. Ray of light at noon on the shortest day

Ernst Studer, church interior in Sarnen (1961–1966)

The targeted study of the phenomenon of space is comparatively new —not its production, but its theoretical examination. Only two exponents[4] are named here: On an urban scale, Camillo Sitte published his book *Der Städtebau nach seinen künstlerischen Grundsätzen* ("Urban planning according to artistic principles") in 1889, above all examining urban space. A few years later, August Schmarsow pointed out in texts and lectures that space is a superordinate and independent category and is common to all built and conceived architecture. In his inaugural lecture "Das Wesen der architektonischen Schöpfung" ("The nature of architectural creativity" in 1893, he stated the following: "Spatial sense and spatial imagination urge towards spatial design and seek satisfaction in an art; we call it architecture and could simply call it in German *Raumgestalterin* 'spatial designer').

Only three decades later, in the early Modern period, the idea of function moved into the foreground and was communicated in a dominant trend of Modernism, as if architecture could be exclusively created out of its functions and scientifically developed from them. Theoretical study of space and spatial design receded into the background.[5] It was only prior to Postmodernism, in 1971, that Louis I. Kahn presented his designs and drawing entitled, *Architecture Comes from The Making of a Room*, specifically referring to the indifference between function and space, and the significance of spatial design. Spaces can be equipped with very different qualities and provide the framework for a wide range of living content. In the best case, they are carriers of significance going beyond their utilisation, uplifting "vessels of life".[6] Following our activities in our office and in teaching, we share those convictions and presume in the following discussion that architecture can create inspired bodies[7] or inspired spaces.

Although in architecture, space can denote both urban exterior space and private interior space, due to the complexity involved, we limit ourselves in this text to interior spaces. The starting point is the thesis that space—especially interior space "that surrounds us" and "contains"[8]—is perceptible as an independent object and definitively determines the memory of an architectural building. It makes virtually no difference if it is a non-professional or an expert who remembers the space. Everyone can perceive spaces and find them impressive. Spaces rarely move people due to a structural, technical or functional aspect alone. At least in the case of non-professionals—but also among experts[9]—it is obvious that aspects not connected to architectural history or theory are focused on and that they inspire emotions. Instead, spaces move people in a positive sense due to their direct effect that addresses several senses and often even becomes physically tangible.[10] Designed spaces can inspire great emotion, leave behind a magical impression and embed themselves in people's memory.

Since the beginning of our study of architecture, a series of spaces have impressed us to such an extent that we remember our first encounters with them as key experiences. We would describe these exceptional spaces from different periods—which we will call key spaces below—as powerful. They are characterised by qualities such as good spatial proportions, spatial setting, spatial relationship, supporting structure, materiality, light guidance and mutual harmony. We have selected four such spaces from a large number of possible examples and will briefly describe them from the above perspective, even if the works are widely known and have often been discussed before. Based on their characterisation, key aspects of what we regard as powerful spaces will be made recognisable.

The first key experience was the interior space of the University Church of Sant' Ivo alla Sapienza by Francesco Borromini, which was constructed in Rome between 1642 and 1664. The church has already been extensively discussed from various perspectives. The experience of the interior space can only be explained fully through the way the entrance is dramatised. One enters via the loggia of the elongated Renaissance courtyard of the Palazzo alla Sapienza and the courtyard itself, which was mainly constructed between 1564 and 1630 according to designs by the architect Giacomo della Porta. In a kind of counteraction to the architecturally peaceful and horizontally embedded courtyard, the visitor perceives the vertical dynamism of the interior space on entering the cathedral. Access in the floor plan is provided via the tip of two interlocking, equilateral triangles, or read alternatively, at the corner of a six-pointed star. It is extended with niches created by alternating semicircles and trapezes (with a convex fourth side), giving the impression of an enormous wall depth and creating a great girth, which is at least one and a half times the size of the inserted circle. The pulsating figure is precisely and harmoniously embedded in the overall ground plan and the orthogonal framing. The 18 pilasters of the colossal order structure the spatial sequence; with the exception of the three pairs in the apses, they occupy the inner and outer corners of the projections and recesses, while the distances between them remain unchanged.

The connection between the church spaces and the dome space is ambiguous, since on the one hand a clear distinction is articulated by a shaded cornice. The separating effect is enhanced by the tectonics of the pilaster structure expressing gravity and grounding, as well as the contrasting, hovering and heavenly vault structure—creating an effect like a bloated tent—that is illuminated much more brightly. On the other hand, the continuation of the pilasters of the church space with its venations in the dome space creates an overall form and a coherent flow of forces from the ground to the zenith of the dome, which is additionally supported by the immediately white,

4   Nevertheless one important author should be noted with respect to space: Hermann Sörgel: "Wesen der Architektur als raummässige Kunst", in id., *Einführung in die Architektur-Ästhetik. Prolegomena zu einer Theorie der Baukunst*, Munich 1918, p. 148–172.
5   See Sina Keesser: "Räume und Grenzen – Der Raumdiskurs in Architekturzeitschriften zu Beginn des 20. Jahrhunderts", at: http://www.archimaera.de/2012/grenzwertig/raeumeundgrenzen.
6   Sokratis Georgiadis: "Nachruf auf Aris Konstantinidis", in *Werk, Bauen+Wohnen* No. 1/2, 1994, p. 65.
7   Cf. Heinrich Wölfflin, "Unsre leibliche Organisation ist die Form, unter der wir alles Körperliche auffassen", in id.: *Prolegomena zu einer Psychologie der Architektur*. Berlin 1999, p. 15.
8   Bruno Zevi, "Wie lernt man Architektur", in *Du* No. 11, 1960, p. 75.
9   Two exmaples can be named here: Adolf Loos reveals his enthusiasm for the interior space of St. Stephen's Cathedral in Vienna, calling it "the most beautiful interior space: St. Stephen's Cathedral". In "Beantwortung einer Rundfrage" (1906), in id., trotzdem. Vienna 1982, p. 62, Aldo Rossi also describes his associations with respect to the atirum at the University of Zurich: "finally, I associated it with an enormous greenhouse. I pictured before me the university with the Invernardero, the palm tree house in Barcelona, with the gardens of Seville and Ferrara, where I can perceive almost complete silence." [trans.] In *Wissenschaftliche Selbstbiographie*, Bern 1991, p. 23.
10   See Karen Michels, *Vollkommene Räume. Orte der Harmonie und ihre Geschichten*, Wiesbaden 2016.
11   "The material in which Borromini's formation is conceived is not a specific, actual substance," [trans.] in Hans Sedlmayr, *Die Architektur Borrominis*. Hildesheim 2008, p. 43.

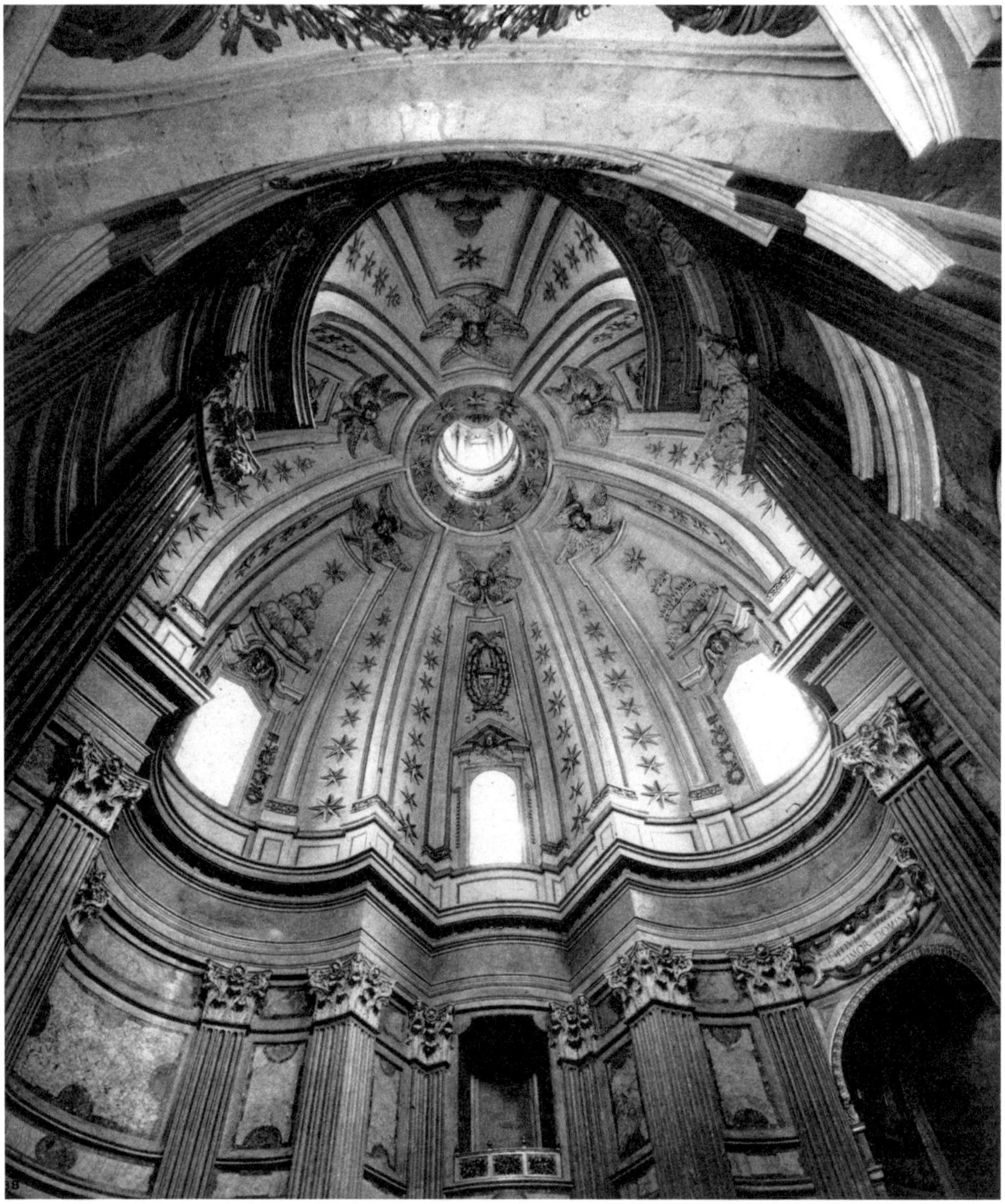

immaterial surface of the stucco.[11] The tambour on the apex, which acts as a skylight, follows the principle of a clear form and also crowns the space. The controlled, logical geometry and section are countered with a sculptural imagination that makes one forget the underlying logic.[12] The individual architectural elements are inscribed into the spatial figure, since the interior is modelled as a sculptural whole.[13] The cupola's form places the spatial structure in the tradition of domed buildings, but at the same time, the complex structure is strongly modified. The interior space of Sant' Ivo becomes a means of advertising the Catholic Church and conforms with the Counter-Reformation principle of overwhelming spaces.

As our second example, we select the office hall of the Johnson Wax Company administrative building in Racine, which was built in 1939 by Frank Lloyd Wright. The drama of the entrance is blatant: starting with a covered drive, the entrance surprisingly merges into the magnificent office hall. It consists of six times ten mushroom columns that appear to oscillate due to their narrower form at the base. The mushrooms are partially fragmented and connected either to a closed ceiling or to translucent glass tubes. The overriding qualities lie in the way the space recalls traditional typologies, which however are simultaneously questioned and reinvented. In this way, the regular structure recalls the column hall of a mosque and similar spatial types with their characteristic impression of an endless expanse of space. It is enclosed outside by a surrounding wall that is rounded at the corners. Between the upper edge of the wall and the bottom edge of the roof, for the first time in architectural history, filtered light penetrates the space, exactly "where the building would usually become heaviest due to the cornice".[14] At the same time, the impression is created of a basin-like space that evokes similar associations in different visitors independently of each other, moving us deeply not only as architects or art historians. It is as if one sees the sky from the bottom of an aquarium: "… we look into the light, like fish from the bottom of a pond," and, "the upper rounded disks recall the leaves of enormous water lilies that appear to float between the glass tubes."[15]

As a third key space, we have chosen the main space of St. Anna's church in Düren (1951–1956) by Rudolf Schwarz.[16] The building volume is based on a three-storey L-shape that is completely closed towards the north and east and presents itself as an enormous stone cuboid. A polygonal, single-storey body is inserted at the "knee hollow" of the form, creating the transition to the church space in the interior through the entrance wall and its series of supports and inspiring various emotions. The low ceiling of the space and the sparse daylight over the cambered glass brick skylights combine with the diagonal concrete ribbed roof to evoke a sense of being beneath the earth. At the same time, one catches a glimpse into the church space,

12 Siegfried Giedion, description of Sant' Ivo entitled "Verbindung von Geometrie und Imagination" in id., *Raum, Zeit Architektur – Die Entstehung einer neuen Tradition*. Zurich/Munich 1984, p. 95.
13 "In his work, a creative spirit is evident that combines methodical architectural insight with the living holistic conception of the sculptor, two talents that were incongruous in the 16th century." [trans.] In Martin Raspe, *Das Architektursystem Borrominis*, Munich 1994, p. 134.
14 Bruno Zevi, *Frank Lloyd Wright*. Zurich/Munich, p. 156.
15 Siegfried Giedion in *Raum, Zeit Architektur – Die Entstehung einer neuen Tradition*. Zurich/Munich 1984, p. 271.
16 The spatial analysis by Thomas Hasler is impressive in id., *Architektur als Ausdruck – Rudolf Schwarz*. Zurich/Berlin 2000, p. 223–243.

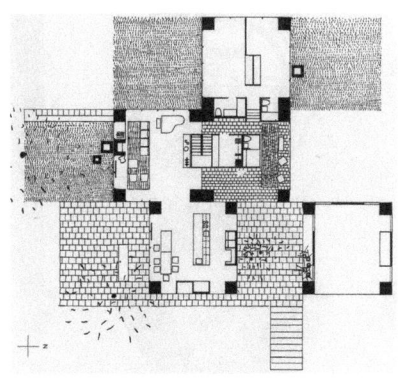

Louis Kahn, ground plan of Adler House, Philadelphia (1954–1955)

Opposite:
Franceso Borromini, Sant'Ivo alla Sapienza, Rome (1642–1664)

with solid stone walls that are illuminated in a celebratory way by the gigantic area of glazing around the corner, which however cannot be seen. In terms of typology, the angular church space recalls a fragment of a Gothic crossing and is characterised by the diaphanous wall, which radiates translucently and allows no views outside. The space is read as a latent image in which the church space is an angular space or an orthogonal, large overall space, into which a mighty, heavy glass volume penetrates, pressing the single-storey entrance area together beneath its load. Every second support in the main space is slightly thicker and transforms into two undergirders of the diagonal concrete ribbed ceiling, thereby giving the space a strong structure. One striking detail is formed by the lintel beams of the corner window, which remains at the bottom edge of the ceiling and thereby has a high point of light and enables the effect of a structural opening. The proportions and structure of the spaces evoke strong emotional, associative and physical sensations—not as a result of analytical observation, but because it makes tangible what Rudolf Schwarz states with his seven "plans"[17] in *Vom Bau der Kirche*: the basic constellations of elementary spatial parameters—in this case set in an image.

The fourth spatial creation with which we connect a key experience is the Yale Center for British Art (1969–1974) by Louis I. Kahn. The cuboid shaped building is four storeys high and consists of six times ten squares with approximately 6-metre edges, which form modular cabinets. To enter the courtyard, one moves diagonally through a compressed entrance zone with four quadrants. Two courtyards have been hollowed out in the symmetrical axis of the strict grid system: the four-storey square entrance courtyard and the second, three-storey courtyard with six quadrants, into which a fair-faced concrete cylinder is set as a sculptural staircase. Above the third storey, a curved grid of concrete girders allows zenithal light to enter. The height of the girders, which have triangular cross-sections, is equivalent to about half a storey, so they can also bridge up to three grid fields in the courtyards without requiring supports and are adequate for the courtyards' spatial proportions. In the single-storey attic, this creates small individual cabinet houses with a roof. The concrete structure with its supports and ceiling is filled in with oak, into which the windows are inserted locally. By hanging large-scale paintings in both courtyards, the windows become the equals of the paintings and also images themselves. The non-supporting partition walls on the top floor open up a passage to the supports from one or both sides. This creates diagonally experienced enfilades, as well as complex views beyond the courtyard and into the spatial diagonals.

The building's stringency and the effective exceptions reveal a high potential for spatial relationships. The architectural language is based on a clear material grammar with a concrete grid structure and exterior fill-ins of sheet steel, a supporting structure and oak fill-ins for the interior, as well as linen-spanned partition walls on the top level. At the same time, the level of the large, urban, second courtyard is combined with the associations of intimate living rooms with gold-framed paintings on oak walls, large Persian carpets and lush flanking leather sofas. The building technology is guided close to the elevator core in two voluminous columns in the symmetrical axes and is naturally integrated into the space and architecture. Louis Kahn was one of the few architects to show how the infrastructure can also be consciously integrated as a design theme into the architecture.

The four spaces used here as examples are also characterised by their highly skilled treatment of the load-bearing structure, for instance in structuring the space (Yale Center), appearing to overcome it using hinged supports (Johnson Wax Building), hovering as an illuminated body (St. Anna), or in the presented tectonics that transform into heavenly spheres in the vault (Sant' Ivo). The examples also show very clear stances with respect to materiality, by maintaining a material dialectic between a visible concrete structure and oak in-filling (Yale Center), a supporting natural stone wall and hovering glass brick walls (St. Anna), dancing concrete columns and clad brickwork walls (Johnson Wax Building), or by unifying the material in stucco for the sake of light guidance (Sant' Ivo). All spaces use the means of compression and relief when entering them, inspiring a physical sensation. All spaces share the fact that they cannot be completely perceived at a glance and have to be walked through. This can be seen in an exemplary way in Sant' Ivo, where the interior cannot be captured on a single photo. All four spaces overcome the fulfilment of their pure functions and seek to use additional aspects to achieve a higher value of utilisation. This occurs in a lively Baroque style (Sant' Ivo) or through the spherically illuminated church space (St. Anna), to impress believers, through the exemplary exhibition of British art (Yale Center), or to introduce the hall type to the office activities (Johnson Wax Building) of modern people.

As a result of key experiences with the four above-described and other key spaces, long-lasting memories and subsequent analysis, our interest in the idea of "powerful" spaces has grown. At the same time, synonyms such as "powerful", "self-confident", "robust" or "durable" come to mind. Although we strive to investigate the term and make it tangible, its unfocused nature will remain. That is not just a flaw, but perhaps the source of their magic. All key spaces ultimately share the fact that they have *overwhelmed* us. To be able to appropriate the phenomenon for our own work, we must limit the wealth of qualities to a few in our own designs. In doing so, the visible image of the load-bearing physics expands to the aspect of the

17 Rudolf Schwarz, *Vom Bau der Kirche*. Heidelberg 1947.

Louis I. Kahn: Architecture comes from the Making of a Room, 1971

Atrium in the main building of the University of Zurich

18 See also Siegfried Giedion, "Die Aufgabentrennung von Architekt und Ingenieur", in Giedion 1984, p. 157–159.

Opposite:
Frank Lloyd Wright, Johnson Wax Headquarters, Racine, Wisconsin (1936–1939)

supporting structure. The well-proportioned simplicity or multifaceted aspect of the space with an equality of mass and emptiness leads to an impressive *spatial figure*. The spatial figure can be grasped below as the *corpus* (Latin) or body (English) and thereby as an indivisible unity. If we add physical aspects or materiality, the term *voluminosity* is introduced. These three aspects of *supporting structure*, *spatial figure* and *voluminosity* enable a simplified, but helpful characterisation of powerful spaces and are discussed in detail below.

Supporting structure

On this planet, the laws of physics force us to apply the laws of developing viable systems. One can regard these underlying conditions as a limiting burden or a liberating opportunity to design them in an innovative way. In doing so, we can give gravity a simple, easily grasped expression, or attempt to overcome it or conceal it. To clarify this relationship between space and the supporting structure, a brief recourse to history is helpful. Until the end of the 17th century, the building was mostly constructed by master builders who fulfilled the spatial and load-bearing construction tasks in an integral way, using their experience and empiricism. For instance around that time, training in France began to distinguish between architects and engineers. In 1794, still during the French Revolution, the Ecole Polytechnique was founded in Paris to develop and communicate the emerging science's technical insight. A completely different programme was launched in 1806 by Napoleon with the Ecole des Beaux-Arts, which celebrated the Baroque yearning for the unity of architecture and art and taught architecture as the "art of building".[18]

As a result of these parallel forms of training, engineers focused on the supporting structure and its technical aspects, while architects mainly limited themselves to questions of the building's form and style. However, both the supporting structure and the architectural expression are on equal terms as means of forming space. There was a danger that architectural space would no longer be regarded, developed and formed in an integral way as an overlap between design and engineering. But it is precisely the discipline of space that is incompatible with one-dimensional observation, instead forming a field of themes that must take all spatially definitive elements, phenomena and disciplines into account. Excluding certain aspects or limiting oneself to individual aspects involves the risk of not fully exploiting the potential of spatial design. While in former times, spatial formation was conceived and implemented by one person, namely the master builder, it must today be sought and developed in early interdisciplinary collaboration between the architect and the planning

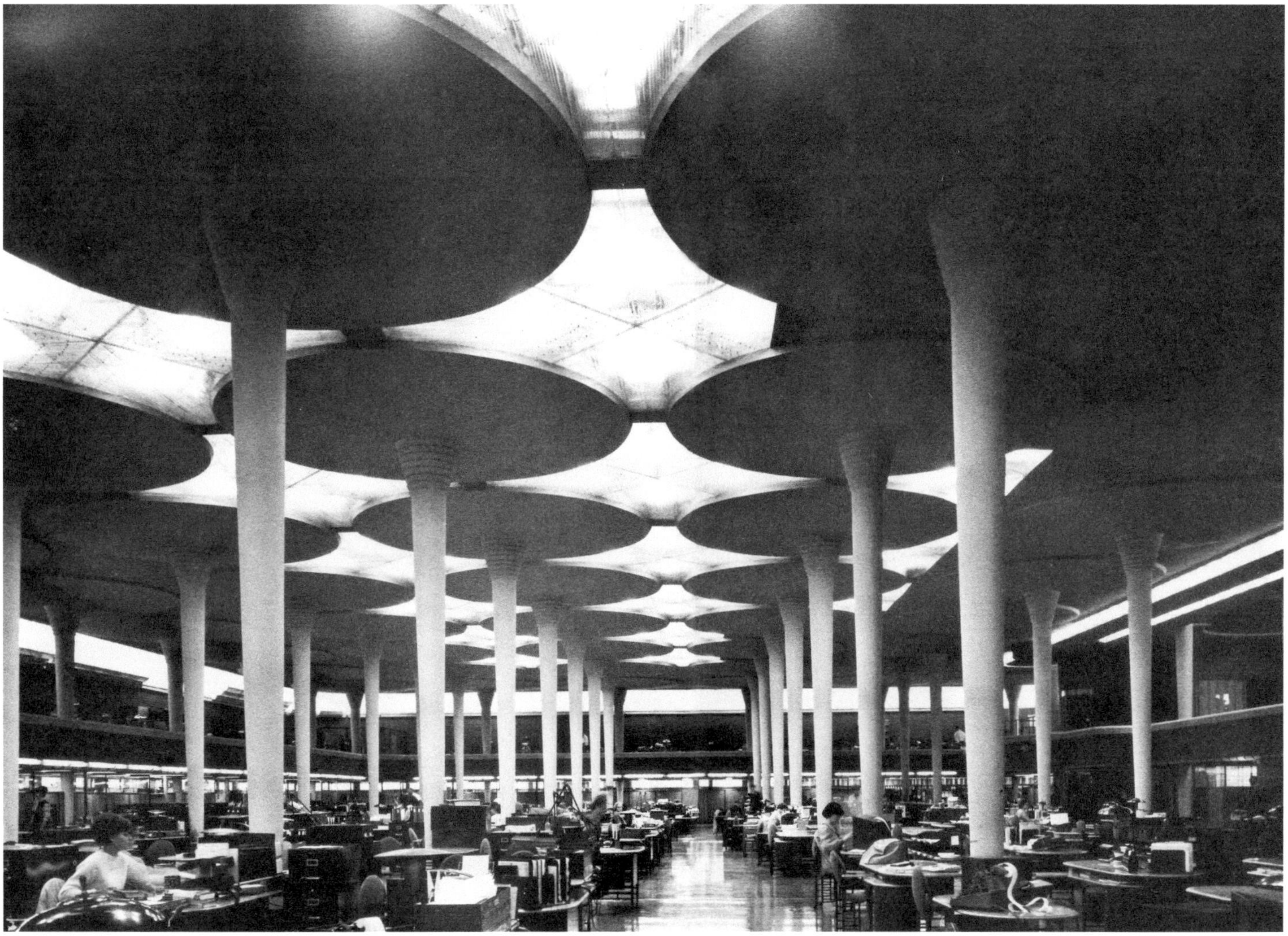

structural engineer. We have sought such an open, non-specialised approach from the very start of our office activities and in teaching in order to do justice to the discipline of space. To this day, a working method of dialogue is evident in numerous cooperations between engineers and architects even after the 18th century.

However, despite a common basic approach, conceptual differences can be seen in practice today.[19] One can divide them in a simplified way into three cases: in the first case, once the architectural design has largely been characterised, the architect seeks a suitable supporting structure with which to implement it. Depending on requirements, the supporting structure may include innovative technology. The primary spatial or building form, or the architectural idea requires a genuine solution from the supporting structure. The load-bearing behaviour serves it. It is not self-explanatory, but complex and occasionally it seems to overcome gravity and undo it locally. In the second case, architecture and the supporting structure are developed together in parallel. A pure and clear conception of the load-bearing structure is a joint priority of the architect and the structural engineer, and is their focus. The building serves to stage the supporting structure as a first-class, timeless means of expression of architecture and resists the threatening impulse to clad the interior or exterior. In the third case, the planner of the supporting structure is involved in discussion together with other participating planners from the outset in developing a design idea. The supporting structure is spatially formative, but not necessarily in the foreground. It is not an end in itself, but instead a definitive means of designing spaces with character due to its design potential. The spatial and supporting structure can be interlocked in a way that allows different readings. The focus lies on space and spatial design without primary staging of the supporting structure. In our own office activities and teaching, we advocate the second and third approaches.

Spatial figure

The term spatial figure contains a paradox, since space describes an emptiness and figure refers to an object with design qualities, which initially seems incompatible. The term only becomes logical and indeed very clear if one imagines making a cast of the interior and assessing and observing it as a sculptural form.[20] It is almost self-explanatory that the inner emptiness must be formed as a vessel and strongly contrasts with the propagated "spatial flow" of Modernism, whereby the exterior space is unlimited and spreads centrifugally. Instead, with its emptiness and centripetal centre, the spatial figure shares with classic spatial types the idea of a strong containment. Unlike these, the openings within a spatial figure are rarely classic windows perforating the wall, and are instead structural, specially aligned openings that enable an inner spatial continuum. The boundary between the interior and exterior is preferably not a membrane, but a spatial zone with its own incremental transition. Interior and exterior spaces are seldom congruent, creating a kind of complex *poché*.[21]

To allow an enclosed emptiness to work and enhance its value, it must largely be surrounded by mass.[22] The mutual precondition of space and body is an exciting relationship of two equal counterparts that comes very close to the sculptural themes of Eduardo Chillida.[23] Both emptiness—as a virtual sculpturally removed mass—and the mass itself have figurative qualities. Precisely in this sense, the term figure is not only a simple stereometric body.

Even in our first competitions for public building tasks, we studied and were interested in spatial figures. Such spatial figures could enclose various fields of use. In the case of spaces that served to provide access, corridors, stairs and entrance halls could be connected to create continuous spatial figures. Large-scale spaces with flexible uses such as spaces for encountering, exhibitions or foyers can create spatial figures. In individual cases, utility spaces with clear functions could also form a spatial figure. Generally, larger spaces covering several storeys are primarily suitable, such as halls or atria. But why did this idea of a spatial figure pursue us, and what can such a spatial figure achieve apart from spatial ambivalence?

Within a complex spatial structure, it s possible to use a comprehensive spatial figure to provide a hierarchy for a spatial programme with a large number of different spaces. In our university buildings, we distinguish between public access and gathering spaces, and chamber-like, more private workspaces. That creates an incremental transition from the public space of the city to the public space inside and on to the private interior. The boundary of the city thereby no longer lies at the outer shell, but is extended into the interior using transitional spaces.[24] Yet the spatial figure also enables rich and exciting spatial relationships. The direct opposition between a spatial figure and introverted private interior spaces can lead to unusual and surprising encounters between activities and people. Like urban spaces such as streets and squares, inward and outward views are created, allowing direct communication.

The spatial figure is situated inside the building. It creates locations for gathering, encountering and communicating, and is characterised by specific qualities with respect to space, light, acoustics and climate. It thereby creates an unmistakeable identity. As such, it can be compared to the organ of an animal—organically as the heart or

19 An interview by Aita Flury with the engineers Muttoni, Schnetzer and Schwartz on the theme of the supporting structure and space is enlightening and insightful, in *Werk, bauen+wohnen* No. 5, 2009, p. 40–47.
20 Luigi Moretti: "Strutture e sequenze di spazi", in *Spazio* No. 7, 1952/53, p. 9–19; or Rachel Whiteread with her sculptures *Ghost* (1990) and *House* (1993).
21 Colin Rowe / Fred Koetter, "Pocher wäre dann das Verpacken oder das Umgeben einer (idealen) Form mit Gewebe", in id., *Collage City*. Basel/Boston/Stuttgart 1984, p. 114. The term *poché* is explained very clearly Robert Venturi, "Innen und Aussen", in id., *Komplexität und Widerspruch in der Architektur*. Braunschweig/Wiesbaden 1978, p. 105–135.
22 On Fuerteventura, the Basque artist Eduardo Chillida hollowed out Mount Tindaya to create his inner "Museum for the Mountain", in which visitors experience the "space of emptiness" in natural light from two vertical shafts.
23 Eduardo Chillida, "When I finally reach my goal, give me some kind of a sign... everything is inseparable now, the space and form that has enclosed him." [trans.] In *Chillida*. Zurich 1981.
24 The merging of urban and architectural space is addressed in Giambattista Nolli's plan "Nouva Topografia di Roma" from 1748. He shows the city as a building mass, whereby specific buildings such as the Pantheon and various sacred buildings are presented as empty vessels in their ground plan and thereby depicted as part of the urban space.

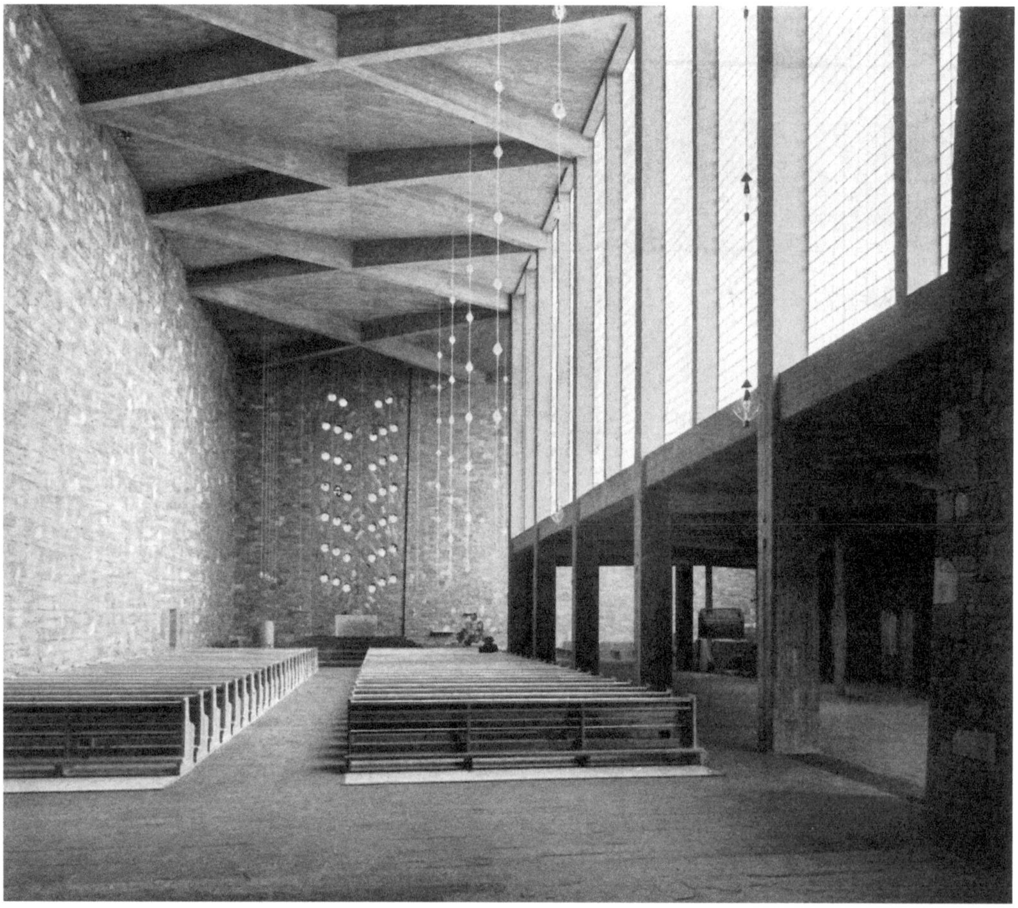

symbolically as the soul of the building. Especially in the case of public buildings, the spatial figure, like the building's appearance, can support the self-presentation of an institution. Not least, a spatial figure creates the opportunity, especially with institutional buildings with diverse spatial uses, to find an independent solution for uses and the location by alienating classic building typologies. Classic urban building types with atria or hall spaces, as constantly used in urban architecture, could combine with special aspects of the programme or location to achieve autonomous, unmistakeable solutions.

A spatial figure is created when the space—be it in the ground plan or the sectional view—forms a harmonious, but complex unity. It should be legible in multiple ways as a multifaceted form[25] or as a coupling of empty volumes. The space can no longer be completely grasped, yet evokes varying spatial conditions, relationships and movement. It is therefore clear that such ambivalent interior spaces cannot be comprehended by viewing it from a single perspective, but only thorough extensively walking through it,[26] since this is the only way to make the drama tangible that is apparent in an on-site visit and in ideal cases manifests itself as a physical sensation. Using contrasting means such as surprising spatial proportions and dimensions, with compressed or expanded roof heights, it is possible to force views upwards into the heights, inspire a sense of plunging, making heaviness or lightness physically tangible.

Voluminosity

Voluminosity is a counterpart to the figuratively formed spatial figure and describes the quality of a sculptural mass that is physically and uniformly shaped like a body, i.e. does not consist of independent individual parts. It creates a simultaneity between the physical quality of a space and the body of the observer, since architecture is characterised by the ability to walk through it. As an indirect appearance of the interior spatial body, voluminosity also refers to construction and material. Therefore our theme is related to plasticity[27] for our understanding of architecture as an organism. There is a widespread opinion[28] that construction and materiality should be subsequent to the development of spatial concepts and form. That affords them less intrinsic value and they are regarded as exchangeable. Construction and materiality are definitive elements of a developed harmony in space—be it interior or urban. The former calls for plasticity and homogeneity and does not want to be divided into its constituent elements such as the wall, floor, ceiling, supports and filling. The spatially formative elements should form an inseparable unity from

25 See Colin Rowe / Robert Slutzky, *Transparenz*. Basel 1997.
26 Fernand Pouillon on the Le Thoronet monastery: "We find that the dynamism of spaces is created by the movement of our heads when walking through them. It is like observing a sculpture on the sculptor's revolving stool. During the movement, we experience the sculptural forms from the outside. Inversely, we experience spaces by moving our bodies within them." [trans.] *Singende Steine*. Munich 1999, p. 157–158.
27 Juhani Pallasmaa's "Six Themes for the next Millennium" (1994) with its "Theme 2, Plasticity" demands that "architecture must learn again to speak of voluminosity, gravity and the self-created logic of tectonics" [trans.], in Fritz Neumeyer, *Quellentexte zur Architekturtheorie*. Munich 2002, p. 569.
28 The distinction between conception and implementation becomes manifest in the increasing splintering of performance in architecture, building management and construction, which is often taken over by specialist firms or general/total contractors.
29 Jacques Lucan, "Hypothèse pour une spatialité texturée", in *matières* No. 9, 2008, p. 6–17.

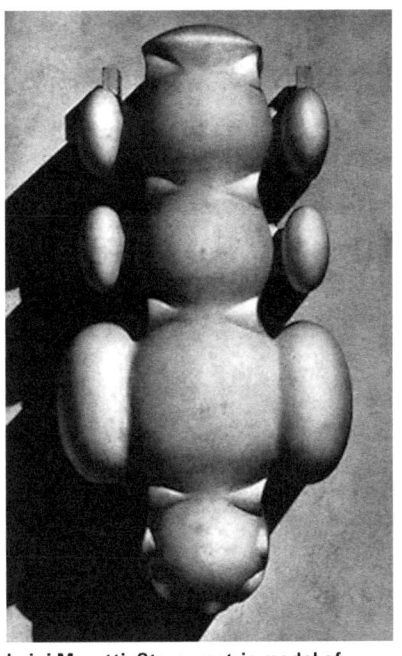

Luigi Moretti. Stereometric model of Guarino Guarini's design for Santa Maria della Divina Providenza in Lisbon

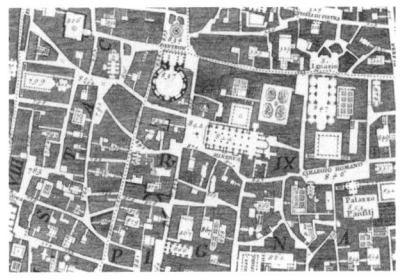

Giambattista Nolli: Extract of the 1748 plan

Opposite:
Rudolf Schwarz, Church of St. Anna, Düren (1951–1956)

30 In the lecture to mark the exhibition opening and book vernissage *giuliani.hönger – dreidimensional* at the ETH Zurich in 2006.
31 Gewicht, "Constructive development, daily concentration and efforts tell me more than the playfully extravagant, more than the striving for the ethereally spiritual," [trans.], in Richard Serra, *Schriften, Interviews 1970–1989*. Bern 2008, p. 208.
32 In the case of complicated buildings, there are often two owners: of the "core and shell" and of the "infill". The infill is inserted as an independent layer into the shell construction and normally clads the enveloped structure.

Detail of a sculpture by Eduardo Chillida

Eduardo Chillida. Project "lugar para todos los hombres", Mount Tindaya, Fuerteventura (1996)

Opposite:
Louis Kahn, Yale Center for British Art, New Haven (1969–1977)

which nothing superfluous can be removed, as Jacques Lucan precisely defined with the term *Espace texturé*.[29]

If the materiality of the wall, floor and ceiling is homogenised and developed in a joint-free way, the room can also be perceived in a mirrored way in its cross-section. Lucan[30] vertically mirrored a photograph of the atrium of the Sihlhof University of Applied Sciences and showed that up and down are interchangeable. In a similar way, we are interested in the inevitability of the relationship between mass and emptiness, and between the figure and the ground. The conventional perception of space is alienated, one's sense of balance becomes insecure and that creates a sense of hovering and an ambivalence and simultaneity of visual weight[31] and weightlessness that can characterise a powerful space. Large spans and projections polarise the ambivalent effect that alternates between "heavy" and "hovering".

At this point we must refer to a current, incisive development. In the past, for example in Gothic architecture, in classical Modernism and even later in buildings such as the Centre Pompidou by Piano und Rogers (Peter Rice planned the supporting structure), the supporting structure could appear outside and inside, and be used in a way that defined the form. Since the oil crisis, the will to achieve a consistent, homogenous structure has been undermined by increased demand for greater diversity, energy efficiency and sustainability. The supporting structure can hardly be located outside any more, must mostly be placed inside and can in best cases form and define the interior spaces, which as can be seen in countless examples in architectural history.

Due to new requirements such as fire safety and acoustics, increasing building technology and investor models such as "core and shell"[32], the visibility and expressiveness of the supporting structure are also endangered inside, since such developments lead to the increased use and presence of wall and ceiling cladding. Undermined by the struggle of architects to achieve a plausible expression for their structures and in view of these changes, tectonics are fading away even inside the building. A "lack of" tectonics, however, can partially be compensated by plasticity using homogenous materials and an appropriately detailed finish, by deliberately shaping neuralgic key points. In the floor plan, it is the projecting and recessed spatial corners, in the section it is the transitions from the wall to floor and ceilings, in incisions, the transitions from the wall to the underside and the reveal: in these places the material should cover both sides of a corner, so that the material thickness remains concealed, allowing one to focus on the voluminosity.

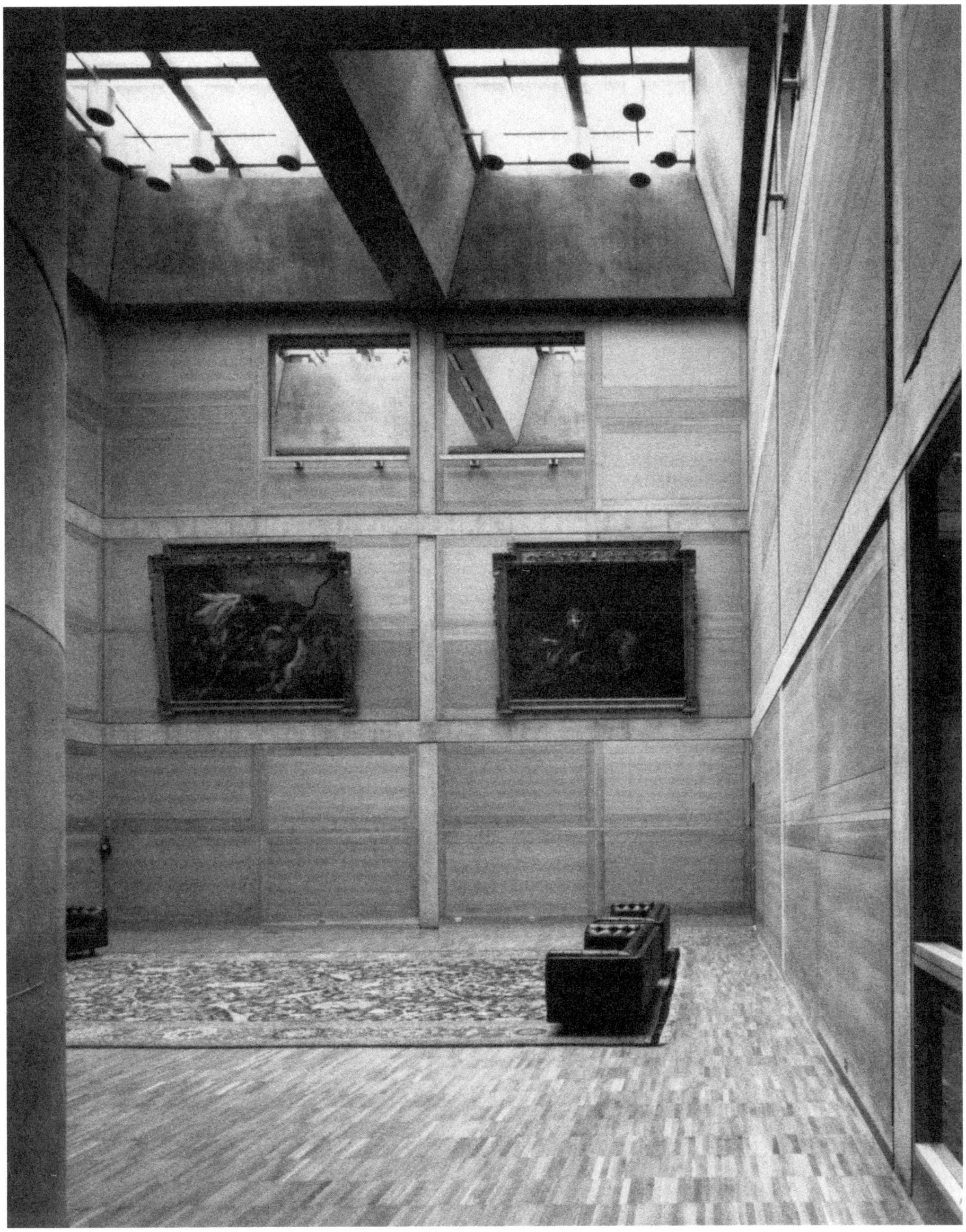

Teaching

Space is a connecting, intercultural and transtemporal motif in all societies. We are all directly affected since we spend most of our lives, work and leisure in such spaces. Memories and dreams, literature and films take place in spaces. The fact that spaces have a key effect on us and we reproduce them often unconsciously as a society is too often overlooked. As professionals, we therefore have a duty to develop knowledge of space as a central architectural phenomenon and offer strategies to develop powerful and unmistakeable spaces.

After two decades of office activities and over a decade of separate design teaching at Universities of Applied Sciences, the teaching opportunity in Lausanne offered us the chance to jointly develop a design course. We were able to provide a sensible complement to the focus study of the material of concrete[33] with interests and themes relating to our own work. Our long-term investigation and study of both—the material concrete and the theme of space—in competitions, built projects and previous teaching, formed an appropriate background experience and provided the required competence.

Due to positive experiences in our collaboration with inspired structural engineers[34], it was clear from the outset that we also wanted to integrate an expert on supporting structures[35] as a Lecturer into our teaching. Specifically the aspect of planning the supporting structure appeared to us to be especially appropriate to also approach architectural design in an interdisciplinary constellation at the university. Perspectives and themes of architecture and of the supporting structure should be combined at the stage of initial design approaches to achieve as homogenous a spatial formation as possible.

Going beyond the specific design tasks themselves, the year-long courses were structured in two superordinate themes, so that students studied "urban constellations" in the respective spring semesters and "powerful spaces" in the autumn semesters. Regardless of the spatial programmes of the project tasks, they studied the themes of supporting structure, spatial figure and voluminosity, thereby developing their own views of the three aspects. The diversity of the solutions found and the passionate engagement with the entire teaching team was very pleasing. Thus in this context, the theme of "powerful spaces" is the content of this publication, since we believe it is a specific theme worth discussing that can serve current architectural teaching. Within this search for powerful spaces, aspects such as creating publicity and privacy inside a building, the identity of a building and an institution, unifying spatial and supporting structures, developing iconographic spatial forms and the search for appropriate material application—especially concrete—were all integrated.

---

33 Extract from the semester programme: "The term Concrete Architecture should be grasped in more ways than one, since it explicitly also addresses the conceptual approach of the course: It seeks innovative, distinct spatial concepts in concrete, which are also feasible and realizable in "concrete" with respect to the load-bearing structure, construction and materials. At the same time, we see the design process itself as an analogy to the concrete production process: Design ideas are fed through the process of forming, casting, condensing and hardening."

34 The engineering offices Dr. Joseph Schwartz Consulting, Zug, or Dr. Lüchinger+Meyer, Zurich, were mostly involved in our courses.

35 Projects were participated by Dr. Massimo Laffranchi from Fürst Laffranchi Bauingenieure, Aarwangen.

On a spatial category in the work of Giuliani Hönger and the design studio Powerful Spaces

Tibor Pataky

> The room is a marvelously sensitive thing. [...]
> The shape is like a personality. Such is the power of spaces.
> (Louis Kahn)

1 Jacques Lucan, "Masse und Textur", in *giuliani.hönger–dreidimensional*. Zurich 2006, p. 11; Lucan uses the term in connection with Olgiati's school building in Paspels, cf. Jacques Lucan, "Textured spaciality and frozen chaos", in *Valerio Olgiati–2G Nr. 37*, 2006.

The relationship between the studio pieces and projects by the office Giuliani Hönger presented in this volume are clear. Experiments are made with design strategies that have been playing a key role in the design practice of teachers for almost two decades. That above all applies to the two designs for academic facilities in Zurich and St. Gallen, and the student designs for the KIBAG administrative building and the shipping yard for ZSG in Wollishofen; as the motto of *Powerful Spaces* already indicates, spaces are the focus of the designs: halls for the shipping yard, courtyard-like spatial structures for the administrative offices. Often, they conform to the task, themes and conceptual perspective according to a special spatial category in the design of Giuliani Hönger, which will be the focus of the following observations.

Sihlhof University of Applied Sciences, Zurich (2000–2003)

The spatial figure as an image

The courtyard for the Zurich University of Applied Sciences, consisting "of interleaving, overlapping, hollowing out and crossings" has been described by Jacques Lucan as an *espace texturé*.[1] Unlike Lucan's formal interpretation, this central spatial figure—and also the Tourism College in Samedan or similarly conceived student works—can be regarded as a response to the conditions of today's building: a reaction initially to the shrinking leeway between the "internal pressure" of maximised spatial programmes and the "external pressure" of limitations to the cubage as a result of legal regulations and budget constraints. In this context, a comparison between Karl Moser's atrium at the University of Zurich and the courtyard of the Zurich University of Applied Sciences is revealing, since Giuliani Hönger name the former as a reference themselves:[2] If one arranged the university courtyards, which are displaced towards each other, as a vertically continuous space in the typological purity of the university building, the considerably more modest spaces would become all the more obvious; the courtyard would assume the proportions of a shaft and the doubled floor space would be lost. In this way, the meandering sectional figure—for both courtyards and their exits on the ground of the surrounding building volume—become an image of the pressure to strive for the maximum spatial exploitation.

The conceptual proximity of such *spatial figures* to what one could summarise with the term described by Heinrich Kulka as the *spatial plan* is by no means of a merely formal nature and is instead connected to the conflicting goal of maximising utilisation and the desire for spaciousness. Not without cause did Loos legitimise "the release of a floor plan in space" on grounds of economy: "But the floor plans were all released on the surface, while I believe the architect should think in space, in a cube. In that sense I was always at an advantage in terms of spatial economy. A water closet does not need to be as tall as a hall."[3] Although Loos is not talking about minimising building volumes or even costs, but instead reflecting on the relationship between use and spatial height: the demand for economy is implicit in the latent functionalism. And the *spatial plan* enables at least the idea of arranging spaces in a more compact—and in that sense more economic—way without any actual loss, since only "superfluous space" is eliminated. And like the *open floor plan*, from which it is applied to the section, this principle becomes more relevant with increasing economic pressure. More important than such optimisations are the gains that are achieved through the alternating openings in the vertically shifted spaces: the visual addition of the spatial depths of the music, living and dining rooms, the seating niches, corridors and stairs of Loos's later villas: not only the functionally required, but also—generally speaking—all the spaces that can be perceived in any way are mobilised.

Especially with the building for the Zurich University of Applied Sciences, the presence of the central courtyard space is maximised: by its angular geometry and the accordingly large "enveloping surface"; due to the bridge that crosses it, through galleries and terraces that touch on it, through windows serving as views outside. The vertical development of the courtyards was therefore also necessary as a precondition for its presence in the overall building. This striving to achieve such a quality—which was not planned in the competition programme[4]—is tangible in the central space. Indeed its significance for the building's interior—as is also the case in the two courtyard-like spaces for the St. Gallen University of Applied Sciences—can hardly be overestimated; initially because the space significantly contributes to orientation in the expansive building volume—both visually and acoustically: because by largely doing without noise-absorbing measures, the increasing or decreasing noise levels in the corridors indicate the direction one is moving in with respect to the hall; secondly and perhaps more importantly: because the courtyard space gives the building interior a face and, like the Moser inner courtyard, creates a recognisable location that also becomes a stage of social encounter. Conceived as a continuation of the public space, its extra height refers to the special importance of its function.

In numerous student pieces and no less so in the case of the Zurich University of Applied Sciences, the relationship between the central spatial figure and the surrounding spaces is dichotomous. It stands in a clear accordance with the figure-ground principle of the sectional views, in which "mass" and "space"—or "texture" in Lucan's terms—are dialectically interlocked. Similarly, in terms of the materialisation and fittings the naked, raw and hard represents the antithesis of completely clad sections—fair-faced concrete and natural stone opposite double-layered plasterboard, fibreglass and linoleum; the homogenous nature of the courtyards and corridors compared to the heterogeneous seminar rooms, meeting rooms and offices; emptiness compared to the furnished and fitted; the tangible spatial edge compared to those concealed by the balustrade channels. Certainly this polarisation is not just the creation of a figure-ground constellation as a formal principle of spatial composition, since it also articulated the different uses of the courtyard-corridor continuum and the cell-like seminar and office rooms. In the case of the Zurich University of Applied Sciences, the different design leeway depending on the utilization category no doubt also played a role; on the one hand the main uses fixed by the spatial programme—highly determined not only in all of its measurements, but also due to regulations, noise, light and ventilation standards, the wishes of the users and client; on the other hand, what was declared as a break area or foyer in the spatial programme and also summed up as the "necessary evil" or an accessing area—which is much more flexible in terms of its expanse and form and much less the focus of the users and client's wishes, as well as regulations (with the exception of fire safety). In this reading, the spatially formative access to the Zurich University of Applied Sciences and many of the KIBAG designs belong to the actual field of architectural experimentation, with respect to the building's interior, not only because halls and courtyards are large and their functions are prestigious, but also due to the higher level of formability.[5] The strategy would be similar to the master plan of OMA / Rem Koolhaas for Melun-Sénart, which was later applied to the Paris National Library: in the chaos of the structurally placed, the inclusions of the unbuilt as a form. Koolhaas stated: "if the built can no longer be controlled, it is rather the control of the void that should be sought."[6]

2   giuliani.hönger–dreidimensional, Zürich 2006, p. 43. Matthias Ackermann also compares the two designs in discussing the work in *Werk, Bauen+Wohnen*, No. 7/8, 2003, p. 27.
3   Adolf Opel, *Konfrontationen–Schriften von und über Adolf Loos*. Vienna 1988, p. 56. Extensively discussed in Fedor Roth, *Adolf Loos und die Idee des Ökonomischen*. Vienna 1995, p. 169–173.
4   During the competition, the maximum building cubature was initially calculated and the required volume according to the spatial programme was then distributed within it. That allowed the volume of the two courtyards to become additional available space. Statement by the architects in a personal conversation.
5   This assumption is supported by the photographs of the buildings' interior spaces and the plans and models of the students' designs, in which the sectional view and the spatial figure written into it are unmistakably the central focus.

Giuliani Hönger, College for Tourism, Samedan (1995–1997)

Irene Wendelin, KIBAG administrative offices, Autumn Semester (2013), concept model

OMA / Rem Koolhaas, model for the Melun-Sénart competition (1987)

Increasing exposure

In the courtyards of the Universities of Applied Sciences in Zurich and St. Gallen, as well as the courtyards and halls of the student works, the fair-faced concrete of the walls and ceilings forms the definitive material for the spatial impression; the rest: natural stone flooring, screen-like spanned acoustic panels, veneered doors. In general one could say that between colour—according to Semper the most immaterial form of cladding—and material, the latter is given priority. Accordingly, the necessary surface protection is minimised, the fair-faced concrete is treated, not sealed and the same applies to the natural stone: as little as possible should be lost of the character of these surfaces, no varnish-like coating upon them. Overall there is a tendency towards a communicativeness—for instance toward coarse or structured elements—that can also be grasped as a form of entering into the specific quality of the tactile sense. Arthur Rüegg and Martin Steinmann have used the term "material colour" in this context, as opposed to the colour of the paint.[7] Similarly, August Schmarsow regarded the term of natural colour, for colours that "are in close connection with the tactile qualities of the bodies."[8] According to Schmarsow, such a perception of colour that corresponds with the tactile experience, has a "more convincing, more urgent" effect than when isolated. He sees the source of that additional effect in the aspect of physical experience that is the special quality of the tactile sense: "In this sensorial effect, it is the material that draws us into the spell of bodily existence."[9] The character of tactile sense and its reference to bodily existence will be discussed in detail below; here the most important aspect is Schmarsow's observation that some of the tactile qualities also inform the eye, which pre-empts it and unfolds an effect that goes beyond a purely visual impression before or even without any touching having actually occurred: "They [the tactile qualities that are also visible] are prioritised because they affect the wider surroundings and yet at the same time, already when seeing, promise the tactile test that actual quality can only be confirmed by a different sensorial sphere. But let us not be mistaken: visibility is only the preferred means with respect to these qualities; the aim remains tactile for a long time; because only it comes so close to us, touches us directly."[10]

As in the case of the Zurich University of Applied Sciences, the visibility of the concrete structure of the courtyard-like spaces in the schemes for the KIBAG administration is an exception with regard to the entire building. In the case of the University of Applied Sciences, it disappears in the rooms aligned along the façades, behind the above-mentioned double-layered façade and the white coat of paint, while from the outside it envelops a multilayered facade. In this way, the courtyard becomes a place where something is possible that would hardly be feasible in the façade and is difficult to achieve in the seminar rooms: showing things unclad—the concrete structure and also the remaining materials that constitute the space. If one compares this solution to those of the academic buildings in Samedan and St. Gallen, which were constructed before and afterwards, one can see an increasing degree of revealing of the spatial enclosure, which is no doubt more than the result of coincidental conceptual agendas: in Samedan (1994–1997), the sculptural spatial figure, which was developed out of the entrance connections, was a brand-new achievement; the spatial figure and classrooms are still treated equally; here and there, the structure disappears behind the all-homogenising plaster. Showing the mixed construction of concrete and brickwork would disturb the coherence of the spatial continuum. In St. Gallen (2003–2013) however, one was able to build on the experiences of the two university buildings, whereby the principles of spatial treatment tested on the Zurich courtyards (2000–2003) could be applied to the outer spatial layers. In the seminar room too, the shell construction is revealed, while the required additional technology is focused on isolated elements that withdraw from the concrete structure and are concluded flush with the spatially formative elements. And just as the figure-ground principle of the Zurich University of Applied Sciences can be read as the conceptual starting point of most KIBAG designs, so can the presence of fair-faced concrete extended to the entire building interior be regarded as the starting point for the students' designs of the ZSG shipping yard.

All the named examples are load-bearing structures of reinforced concrete that are exposed as fair-faced concrete in different measures. However, this "revealing of the load-bearing structure" has little to do with the structural rationalism of Viollet-le-Duc, Perret or Kahn: it is not concerned with the hierarchies of supporting and non-supporting elements or an image of the flow of forces in the joints and details. It is instructive to compare the library courtyard in St. Gallen with Kahn's library courtyard at the Yale Center for British Art, due to a series of striking analogies. In both cases, they have a cuboid courtyard form surrounded by a supporting fair-faced concrete supporting structure, with apertures that are framed by oak wood—almost completely in New Haven and up to the height of the balustrades in St. Gallen—thereby forming an inner façade that clearly conforms with the exterior of the building envelope for structural reasons. The courtyards are covered by supporting grids with cassette-like skylight openings, and only where and when it is unavoidable is the natural light supplemented by artificial lighting. In New Haven, the girders are voluminous and overarch the supports that are flush with the walls. The supports themselves are recessed with respect to the ceiling face, so that the entire structure is organised in a texture of supporting and non-supporting building elements. In the case of the St. Gallen library courtyard, tectonic distinction of any kind is avoided; the ceilings and supports merge to form

6   OMA/Rem Koolhaas, "The End of the Age of Innocence?", in Jacques Lucan, *OMA. Rem Koolhaas*. New York 1991, p. 164.
7   Arthur Rüegg/Martin Steinmann, "Materialfarbe und Farbenfarbe–Zur Gestaltung der Häuser an der Pilotengasse", in *Siedlung Pilotengasse Wien*. Zurich 1992, p. 14.
8   August Schmarsow, *Grundbegriffe der Kunstwissenschaft*. Leipzig 1905, p. 116.
9   Ibid. p. 122
10 Ibid. p. 101

Foyer and seminar room, College for Tourism, Samedan (1995–1997)

a grid, which is however incomplete on three sides: the verticals do not lead to the ground, which initially appears to be arbitrary, until the continuous supports on the foyer side are recognisable as the base of the tower over the supporting grid. However, it remains unclear where the broadly projecting ceilings are suspended, since those supports are concealed from view inside the blocks serving as bookshelves. By contrast, the design of the courtyard for the Zurich University of Applied Sciences is atectonic in its fundamental alignment: initially because the division of tasks between "load-bearing structure and wall-forming filling" is dissolved in a structure that is both supporting and consists of spatially formative disks in accordance with the plate-disc structural principle developed by Fred Angerer.[11] The different levels of supporting requirements—depending for instance on the spans of the walls, which mostly are not situated above each other—and the accordingly varying structural means (local prestressing, different ceiling and wall thicknesses) are in no way reflected towards the courtyard, nor are the broad spans of the suspended ceilings. Instead, the distinction that is so decisive for tectonics between "up" and "down"—which for Kahn also represented the formal grounding of architecture—is consistently covered up, creating the impression that Lucan described as a space that is subtractively cut out of a homogenous mass.

Staircase and lounge, St. Gallen University of Applied Sciences, Zurich (2000–2003)

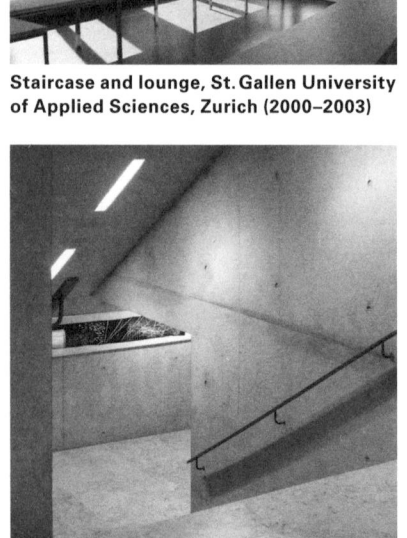

Staircase and seminar room, Sihlhof University of Applied Sciences, Zurich (2000–2003)

The things themselves

But it would be wrong to assume that tectonic perceptions are simply ignored. The hidden supports in the St. Gallen library or the lecture theatre of the University of Applied Sciences in Zurich provoke deliberate irritations and are aimed—albeit with other means—at achieving the same effect as the typological and motif-based alienation of the two courtyards. But where does this interest in alienation and irritation come from?[12] Is it connected to interest in the tactile? Or in more general terms: What can be said about these interests themselves?

"Spaces, like perception itself, mark in the innermost of the subject the fact of his birth, the constant contribution of his corporeality, a communication with the world that is older than thinking. That is the very reason why they fill one's consciousness and remain obscure to reflection."[13] Space in Merleau-Ponty's Phenomenology of Perception is perceived space and not all levels of perception can be distinguished, only those that are directly sensorial and untouched by reflexive consciousness. Methodically it is orientated towards phenomenological reduction based on Husserl: at least initially refraining "from everything that people and sciences believe they know"[14]—in this context Husserl is also speaking of bracketing. The apparently known, which does not belong to the object of observation, is bracketed to reveal the "thing itself" as its essential content and to allow its observation.

In the 1990s, Gernot Böhme applied the strategy of reduction to architectural discourse with his term of atmosphere;[15] in doing so he turns away from the "dominance of semiotics"—i.e. a way of observing architecture that is one-sided in its orientation towards the "model of language"[16]—validating "deeper layers" of spatial experience that are immune to "perceptive socialisation".[17] Practically at the same time, Kenneth Frampton recognised tectonics as an opportunity for architecture to rediscover itself; thus, "the built is primarily a construction", "more a thing than a sign"; to which one could add a reference to Umberto Eco: "even though it is ultimately a mixture of both", which sounds like a concession to the claim of the validity of semiotics, but is meant to be used as a term to oppose tectonics, which their discourse does not address.[18]

These trends within architectural discourse conform with a far-reaching bracketing of signs, quotes and symbols, narrative and discourse in the majority of dominant German-Swiss architecture of the 1990s and 2000s. It applies not least to the oeuvre of Giuliani Hönger; for instance in the case of the Zurich University of Applied Sciences, there is no reference to the design by Karl Moser, which would only have an approximate character of a quote; the type of the courtyard is picked up on in a transtemporal sense. Nor can the grid of the St. Gallen college library hardly be grasped as a design that addresses the theme of rationalistic architecture, and instead must be regarded as a framework of plates and supports, again in a transtemporal sense. Similarly, the use of fair-faced concrete in the courtyard of the Zurich University of Applied Sciences: the motif connection for instance with well-known formwork images with a modular structure, as seen with Louis Kahn and Tadao Ando, is systematically counteracted according to the principle of alienation—through the size and format of the formwork boards themselves, through the rhythm of formwork boards and the joint holes, which are shifted in opposition to each other, and through the staggering of formwork board joints on each floor and the subsequent closure of the joint holes. Indeterminacy remains a characteristic of references, a "referencing" far removed from linguistic coding or explicitness in the sense of Venturi.

However, indeterminacy is a significant characteristic of precisely the consciousness that precedes reflection, namely the most direct perception that is the actual subject of Merleau-Ponty's phenomenological study: "We must decide to recognise indeterminacy as a positive phenomenon. Only in the field of this phenomenon do we encounter qualities. The sense that determines every quality is equivocal, is more a value of expression than a logical significance. The determined quality

11 Discussed extensively in Aita Flury (Ed.): *Zur Zusammenarbeit von Ingenieur und Architekt.* Basel 2011; cf. also Christoph Baumberger, "Tragwerkskonstruktion und Raumgestaltung", in ibid., p.57–71.
12 The "multiple legibility" observed by Christoph Wieser and the ambivalence in the work of Giuliani Hönger can also be interpreted in this direction – when questioned with respect to the effect; cf. *giuliani.hönger–dreidimensional.* Zurich 2006, p. 19.
13 Quoted here and below from the 1966 German edition of Maurice Merleau-Ponty, *Phänomenologie der Wahrnehmung.* Berlin 1966, p. 296.
14 Ibid., p. 11, 13.
15 Gernot Böhme, "Atmosphäre als Grundbegriff einer neuen Ästhetik", in id., *Atmosphäre – Essays zur neuen Ästhetik.* Frankfurt am Main 1995.
16 Gernot Böhme, "Der Glanz des Materials – Zur Kritik der ästhetischen Ökonomie (Vortrag, gehalten am Münchner Designzentrum Dez. 1993)", in id., *Atmosphäre – Essays zur neuen Ästhetik.* Frankfurt am Main 1995, p. 53. Cf. Gernot Böhme: "Anknüpfung – Ökologische Naturästhetik und die Ästhetisierung des Realen". In ibid., p. 13: "If one understands aesthetics to mean the surface, or the presentation, the appearance, the field of the simulacra, then the observation is true that the field of aesthetics has replaced reality. For instance Baudrillard states that today, the world of the fictional already dominates the world of the real. [...] Especially in our times, during the Gulf War, we are learning that reality really exists and that beyond appearances, reality is physical and that the physical remains decisive [...] [trans.].
17 Gernot Böhme: "Über Synästhesien", in *Daidalos* No. 41, 1991, p. 36.
18 Kenneth Frampton, *Grundlagen der Architektur – Studien zur Kultur des Tektonischen.* Munich/Stuttgart 1993, p. 2.

19 Maurice Merleau-Ponty, *Phänomenologie der Wahrnehmung*. Berlin 1966, p. 25.
20 Ibid., p. 366.
21 Cf. Gernot Böhme: "To what extent is material beautiful? / Theories to date let us down if we try to answer this question. Since antiquity, but also in modern aesthetics from Kant to Adorno, the question of beauty has been a question of form." [trans.] In id., "Der Glanz des Materials – Zur Kritik der ästhetischen Ökonomie", in id., *Atmosphäre – Essays zur neuen Ästhetik*. Frankfurt am Main 1995, p. 49. Cf. also Gert Mattenklott: "Das tastende Auge", in Daidalos No. 41, 1991, p. 106–113.
22 Maurice Merleau-Ponty, *Phänomenologie der Wahrnehmung*. Berlin 1966, p. 10.

Louis Kahn, Yale Center for British Art, New Haven (1969–1977)

Library, St. Gallen University of Applied Sciences (2003–2013)

to which empiricism appeals for the sake of definition is an object, not an element of consciousness."[19]

According to Merleau-Ponty, the tactile has a special importance since it is above all tactile experience that cannot be grasped through complete assessment using conscious reflection. Because unlike visual experience for instance, "which drives objectification further than tactile experience," touch, "is connected to the surface of our body; we are not able to spread it out before us, it never completely becomes an object."[20] In the act of touching, perception of one's own body becomes a condition for experiencing that touch in the present. But to appeal to the sense of touch, architecture has the means both of form and of material, so that in the same measure in which the tactile became a means of expression, materiality gains ground on the traditionally privileged form, even if the former is experienced via the diversion of the eye.[21]

The most important premises of this thesis have thereby been outlined: namely those that place interest in the tactile, in alienation and irritation (as modes of the indeterminate), and a reduction that sets all symbolic and narrative in bracketing in the case of buildings such as the Zurich University of Applied Sciences or the St. Gallen University of Applied Sciences, are clearly related to each other, namely in a way that is described by Merleau-Ponty in his Phenomenology. Direct sensory perception, which precedes conscious reflection and has "more expressive value" than "logical significance", would consequently be the actual addressee of this architecture; its intended effect is related to the "amazement" of phenomenological reduction[22] as a recourse to "the things themselves".

Load-bearing structure and spatial formation

On the cooperation between architects and engineers

Joseph Schwartz

Powerful spaces are fascinating to non-experts and experts alike. The breathtaking power of such spaces is inevitably derived from their structure, but ultimately many different aspects contribute to this phenomenon. One key role is played by geometric perspectives such as the scale of the spaces or their proportions. The opening behaviour is also a primary means of light guidance that directly and indirectly supports the spatial quality. All these points are inextricably linked to the load-bearing structure. Often, it is the powerful structures, which are more or less explicitly expressed in the supporting structure, that stage the drama of the load tectonics. Although the supporting structure is an essential element of a building, the question of its presence in architecture still remains valid today. Confrontation between the physical necessity of the work of a structural engineer and the freedom of design that characterises the work of an architect opens up a very interesting field of tension, within which questions of structure and space are central. In this respect, the supporting structure and spatial structure have a direct relationship, since the supporting structure has the role of making the spatial structure physically buildable. Conscious articulation of the statically effective building elements harbours a potential that should not be underestimated in creating powerful spaces.

Chancel of the Beauvais Cathedral (seen from the nave)

Chancel of the Beauvais Cathedral (view from the southeast)

While in antiquity, in temple and cathedral construction, the supporting structure was omnipresent as a structure and also a spatially formative element, it is nevertheless unmistakable that the supporting structure was not only a means to an end in producing such a huge spatial experience, and that the design quality of the exterior appearance becomes completely secondary as a result of the lateral buttresses with which the purity of the phenomenal interior space is achieved. Unlike the cuboid, elementary early Romanesque churches of the Middle Ages, which were inspired by Roman building methods and addressed the theme of the mass and power of the masonry, as well as the enclosed spatial volume, Gothic architecture developed the

Grubenmann Brothers, Church in Wädenswil (interior)

Grubenmann Brothers, Church in Wädenswil (roof model)

concept of handling the material with the aim of dematerialising the walls. The geometry based on sophisticated mathematical calculation led to a functional structure with a building form that contradicts the actual volume and its own weight, thereby creating spaces that embody an independent, transcendental world. In those times, such astounding building achievements were conceived, planned and built by master builders. Long before the job was split into the professions of architect, structural engineer and contractor, highly accomplished buildings were erected, both from a design and a technical perspective, empirically developing sophisticated structures, as well as using building methods that were passed down from generation to generation. Often, the price was high for such a concept or attempting to develop these building methods to perfection, since collapsed buildings during the construction process or shortly after completion were not unusual, unmistakably confirming the limits of mechanics and materials. Instinct and experience were the only means available.

In the 18th century, the carpenter's profession in Switzerland had already attained an exceptionally high status. For example the Grubenmann Brothers showed how the master builder assumed the role of a total contractor including the tasks of architect, structural engineer, material specialist and contractor, producing buildings with baffling speed that still enjoy the highest respect today. Similar building methods were applied in the fields of bridge building and construction: the grown wood allowed the formation of complex spatial, highly efficient supporting structures. For instance in the case of the church in Wädenswil, which was completed in 1867 and is a masterpiece by Johann Ulrich Grubenmann, the entire interior space of the late Baroque reformed church was designed as a transept formed without any supports. The power of the interior space is enhanced in a targeted way by completely concealing the supporting structure, which plays such a central role, and by enhancing the breathtaking spaciousness through the abstract white surfaces with applied decorations, by skilful light guidance, furnishing and the self-supporting galleries. Capitals become ornaments due to the lack of columns, the oval windows create a tension between the rounded transition from walls to ceilings, and the sculptural qualities of the galleries spanning the entire length and breadth of the church are evidence of the enormous technical and design skill of their creator. Not only in this case, but above all in supporting structures for bridges freely spanning areas of 18 × 35 metres over the church space, it becomes especially clear how the master builders knew how to use their great conceptual, constructive and craftsman's intelligence to overcome the limited dimensions of grown wood. The almost profane exterior expression of the building is thus all the more astounding, since it reveals nothing of the audacious interior structure.

After the fields of architecture and structural engineering were separated, with the advent of the industrial revolution in the second half of the 18th century, the profession of engineer gained enormously in status. In the first half of the 19th century, the new material of cast iron was introduced. It was notably used in 1851 for the Crystal Palace planned by the architect Joseph Paxton and the engineer Sir Charles Fox for the Great Exhibition in London. Within 17 weeks, more than 2,000 workers covered an area of 615 x 150 metres in erecting the exhibition hall made of 3,500 tonnes of cast iron and 400,000 panes of glass in Hyde Park. A year later, the Crystal Palace, a kind capitalist manifesto, was dismantled and rebuilt in the London suburb of Sydenham, before being reopened in 1854 as a museum and event location. The building was destroyed by fire in 1936. The modular construction method for a gigantic greenhouse-like hall, which was developed under great economic pressure, allowed the aspects of architecture and the supporting structure to be merged, enabling flexible use and unlimited extension. The lack of scale, combined with a complete lightness and openness, gives the building its exceptional power. The potential of cast iron remained limited, however, due to the difficult qualities of the material, so it was not until the development of wrought iron that the construction of arches and girders with spans of over 100 metres became possible. One such example is the Galerie des Machines, which was completed in 1889 for the Paris World Fair and conceived as a joint project by the architect Charles Louis Ferdinand Dutert and the engineer Victor Contamin. Iron had become fashionable as an architectural material and the discovery of the anonymous engineering skill as a means of design seemed to pave a possible way to developing new architecture that was unlike the hackneyed existing styles, in which the architect and the engineer could be brought together again as joint developers of architecturally articulated structures.

In the fields of construction using reinforced concrete and steel, such advances in theoretical knowledge and technical developments to the materials went hand in hand with a continuous further development of the building methods, which affected not only the supporting structures, but also their construction process. For instance, reinforced concrete construction experienced a transition from bar-shaped construction, based on building with timber, to a monolithic building method, in which there was still a strong hierarchy with respect to the load-bearing elements. The introduction of prestressing allowed greater spans, while also making the structures slimmer; the further development of building materials combined with the economic advantages of the formwork led to supporting structures with monolithic, ever more expansive building elements, composed of interlocking supports, disks, plates and shells. For millennia, the development of buildings was dominated by the question of intuition, empirics and passed-down experience. Only in the last two centuries has it been increasingly

Pier Luigi Nervi, exhibition hall, Turin (interior)

Pier Luigi Nervi, exhibition hall, Turin (building site)

influenced by theoretical aids, enhanced building materials and economic factors. In this context, the developments in Italy before and after World War II are interesting. Pier Luigi Nervi enjoys an exceptional status as an engineer, designer, contractor, material expert and teacher with respect to reinforced concrete. The interaction between his activities led to an oeuvre that goes far beyond the confines of the canon of standard engineering work and architecture. Using specially developed manufacturing methods with prefabricated, very thin formwork elements, Nervi managed to develop his own formal language and apply it with genius to develop and construct powerful spaces. He achieved one highlight in his career with the completion of the exhibition hall in Turin in 1949. A wave-shaped, ribbed dome spans 82 metres over the exhibition space and is structured by lighting perforations and transverse diaphragms. Nervi was convinced that interdisciplinary collaboration between the engineer and the architect was a key condition for the development of powerful spaces, based on balanced, correct constructions combined with excellent design. As a teacher, he thus strived for a long time to combine the two disciplines.

50 years further down the line to our own times, one can detect that despite the almost perfect means and the excellent training in architecture and structural engineering, it remains difficult for the two disciplines to come together and cooperate. The languages are different, there is little awareness of the nature of the other disciplines, and the potential of merging the requirements of both disciplines to achieve a powerful joint design often remains undetected. Nevertheless, there are still buildings in which architecture and the supporting structure regularly merge into each other. For instance in 2001, the architect Toyo Ito won the competition for a media library in Sendai with an extremely poetic design: the prismatic volume consisting of a voluminous network of supports that resemble seaweed dancing in water, as well as floor panels and a façade developed as an envelope. It is not lightness or natural light that are the focus of this building, but the strength of the expression, as is the case with all buildings by Ito. The design is based on a radical dissolution of the distinction between load-bearing and spatially formative elements. The voluminous supports, which serve to provide access to all media and the users, assume not only the vertical, but also the horizontal load-bearing influences. The engineer Mutsuro Sasaki assessed the competition entry as certainly poetic, but far removed from physical reality. He was so fascinated by Ito's idea that he experimented on the idea with models of the bars until he fulfilled both the load-bearing and the aesthetic requirements. The transformation from light sea grass to tree trunks completely changed the dominant design element, as the formerly powerful appearance of the ceilings and the façade envelope receded into the background. The sea grass transformed into a powerful steel structure—and Ito was impressed and inspired by the presence of the bars, which now

resembled objects in a shop window. This is an example of how a powerful basic design idea can be developed into exceptionally powerful spaces through intensive and close interdisciplinary collaboration, whereby a radical transformation from extremely light to much more massive supports proved to be necessary and changed the design greatly, without removing its power.

The Leutschenbach school, which was designed by the architect Christian Kerez in close collaboration with the engineer Joseph Schwartz, impresses with its unshakable unity of material, construction, supporting structure and installations. All struts and supports have a spatially defining function and can thereby only be determined out of the context. The load-bearing concept cannot be distinguished from the architectural and spatial concept. To minimise the developed area of the property, the ground plan was reduced to the smallest possible size, namely the sports hall, stacking all the functions on top of each other, which led to great dependencies from a load-bearing perspective. For instance the rooms with public uses were developed as mezzanines, in which the load-bearing structure withdraws from the façade area and thereby creates a direct reference to the view. The classrooms on three floors and the sports hall are accommodated in the surrounding framework, creating a building out of repeating referential levels. The individual uses were stacked on top of each other with different heights and contrasting floor plan alignments, while maintaining a strong coherence through the uniform material and construction of the supporting structure, ceiling construction and the façade, which is heightened further through the uniform nature of the building method and the integral steel framework. The development of the supporting structure was an intensive, interdisciplinary process, with close cooperation between all those involved in the project. From the first project idea, they worked together to find possible solutions to implementing the underlying concept as efficiently as possible. To give areas such as the administration, assembly hall and library as strong a reference to the public spaces as possible, the floors were largely developed without load-bearing elements on the façade level. Due to their considerable size, both the three-storey classroom body and the sports hall called for the implementation of a broadly projecting body to implement the concept in a plausible way. The situation of the steel framework beams along the façade level was defined using a very time-consuming parameter study that took all the main criteria during the course of the project into account. This decision significantly supported the demand for the individual bodies to be bound together in as powerful a way as possible, yet increased the level of difficultly with respect to the project tasks; not least, supporting the ground floor on only six steel tripods gives the ground floor an exceptional power by staging the hovering building volume above a space with a constricted height and an unlimited outward view.

Toyo Ito, Sendai Media Library (interior view of a support)

Toyo Ito, Sendai Media Library ("glass" model of the load bearing structure)

Christian Kerez, Leutschenbach School, Zurich (ground floor)

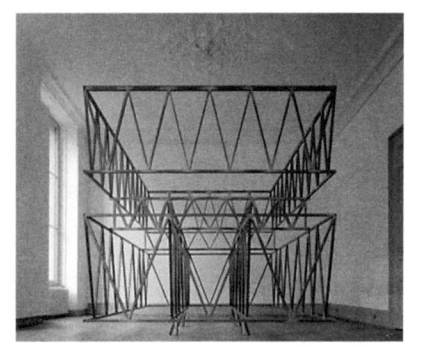

Christian Kerez, Leutschenbach School, Zurich (model of the supporting structure)

The Hilti Innovation Centre in Schaan designed by the architects Lorenzo Giuliani and Christian Hönger in collaboration with Joseph Schwartz is an elongated, extendable base construction that is aligned beneath the existing upper administrative building. The exterior expression is characterised by the horizontal layer of balustrades with different heights —window bands that stage the surrounding panorama and make the desired flexibility of the interior spaces visible. The requirements of the client, namely to pool the production, research and service areas in one building and network them closely, led to an exciting spatial concept in which the supporting structure plays a key role. The two-storey, support-free testing hall is situated in the core of the building. It is surrounded on three sides by conventional skeleton structures in reinforced and prestressed concrete, accommodating the laboratories and office levels. To strengthen the effect of the hall as a connecting element between individual uses, the aerial space is zoned using a grid of longitudinal and lateral single and double-storey girders, which literally appear to hover over the large testing hall and leave atria in the spaces between them. These voluminous connecting bodies span the hall with the help of floor-high steel frameworks in the building's lateral direction between the hall's limiting walls and between the perpendicular longitudinal bridges respectively. The two-storey bridge girders only have frameworks on the upper level, while the lower plate is suspended from the framework girders using diagonal ties. Various uses, including access, common rooms and a large conference room are arranged in the connecting girders. The contrasting spatial principles, lighting moods and materials create ideal conditions in the entire building for focused work, the targeted exchange of ideas within a team and a relaxed visit. The clear load-bearing and secondary structure ensures highly flexible utilisation.

It is undisputed that with respect to designing buildings, the requirements of transdisciplinarity in recent decades have grown continuously. That situation is often presented as a possible reason for the increasing difficulty in collaboration between representatives of the different professional disciplines; thus indirectly, it is also implied as a reason for the increasingly difficult integration of the load-bearing structures in the architectural design. Regardless of whether the supporting structure is shown or concealed, its careful conceptual development is a fundamental condition for the development of powerful spaces. In that respect, it is regrettable that architectural designs by many contemporary Swiss architects begin with images that are then implemented with today's almost unlimited technical means. Nevertheless, in the architectural generation of Lorenzo Giuliani and Christian Hönger, one sees protagonists who make the supporting structure a key design aspect as the generator of the spatial structure. From the perspective of this author, the level of intent and the awareness of integrating the supporting structure vary greatly among the various architects with whom he has worked closely. It is therefore difficult to make an objective assessment, above all since recent collaboration has been with young architects who seek transdisciplinary collaboration in a similar way to Lorenzo Giuliani and Christian Hönger. However the office Giuliani Hönger assumes a special status since in addition to its powerful stance both with respect to urban planning and on materials, it has managed to develop its own approach, especially to large-scale buildings, with respect to the skilful articulation of large spaces, both in the ground plan and in its sectional view. Evidence of such work can be seen in the libraries of the St. Gallen University of Applied Sciences, the new vonRoll building in Bern and the large testing hall of the Hilti Innovation Centre in Schaan, in which without doubt, aspects of design and the load-bearing structure have been merged in a skilful way.

Giuliani Hönger, Hilti Innovation Centre, Schaan (testing hall during construction)

Giuliani Hönger, Hilti Innovation Centre, Schaan (steel girders over the testing hall during construction)

The design studio Powerful Spaces

Student projects, EPFL, 2013–2015

Raphael Dunant, Michael Meier

The design theme of powerful spaces was approached as part of a number of different tasks: administrative offices for the construction material company KIBAG (Autumn Semester 2013), a shipping yard for the Zürichsee-Schifffahrt & Gastro (Spring Semester 2014) and a dance school at the Römerhof (Spring Semester 2015). The selected context was concrete locations in the Zurich region. Complex spatial programmes were defined in advance, in which large spaces or spatial interconnections—if at all explicitly listed—were the exception. While the study of concrete as a building material was another constant thematic focus of all semester designs, the respective uses provided the chance to give the design a distinctive character. The serious, long-term work on a spatial concept was supervised by the Professor and structural engineer Massimo Laffranchi . Seven semester designs are presented here—as a small selection from over 120 projects—demonstrating the breadth of the developed experiments on the theme of "powerful spaces".

Structural density, Jérémie Corminboeuf, p. 50–51

In his project for the concrete producer KIBAG, Jérémie Corminboeuf presented a study of the spatial and architectural potential of a geometrically repetitive spatial structure. A simple diagrammatic underlying principle is the starting point of the design: the sequence of concrete cylinders within a rectangular basic form. This simple structure, which was derived from an industrial silo facility, is structurally and spatially manipulated. The composition and articulation of these measures also form the actual architectural project. Alone or in groups, the large cylinders form spatial compositions. In the intermediate spaces, smaller cylinders are used for the stairs and lifts, for central sources of daylight and for the building technology.

The expressive, dense structure of the joined cylinders forms a dialogue between the empty space, the envelope and the selectively spaced openings to create a characteristic interior space. The spatial chambers within the cylinders are therefore continuously or indirectly connected to each other. The simple conglomerate of basic geometric volumes thereby becomes a structurally developed, flowing, yet locally framed spatial continuum.

Spatial machine, Damien Magat, p. 52–53

Goethe's Sorcerer's Apprentice experiments with a machine. A process determines the scene in a brief poem—dynamism to the point of delirium. An unstoppable machine is described, like the one 150 years later that projects Charlie Chaplin onto the cinema screen.[1] The aforementioned referential world questions dynamic, machine-like phenomena with respect to their order and humanity. The question also seems to be the starting point for Damien Magat's spatially formative experiment: a tall, vertical spatial figure with a simply composed building volume is permeated by the flow of commodities in an industrial production line. Parallel to it, a stairway consisting of mechanical and static steps winds its way through the space.

Magat plies the sense of disorientation and the experience of monumentalism in the belly of a mighty machine. Production, access and exhibition spaces all become one. They form the heart of the modern-day industrial plant: a place like a spatial design that Goethe saw in his contemporary Piranesi.[2]

Monolith, Diogo Veiga, p. 54–55

A robust, yet finely organised spatial sculpture unfolds within an abstract, Cartesian building volume. The cave-like interior space could refer to a glacial origin, were the volume and empty space not so skilfully modelled and detailed with respect to the guidance of light and movement. It is thus an artefact with an archaic appearance. That possibly refers to a medieval understanding of space and structure, as Louis I. Kahn demonstrates in the ground plan drawing of Comlongon Castle.[3] *Poché* is also applied to the sectional figure with the constructive and structural possibilities of reinforced concrete. In addition to Kahn's principle of servant and served rooms, Diogo Veiga's design also appears to refer to the Central Library by his teacher Aires Mateus in Lisbon.

---

1 Modern Times. Film, 1936, directed by Charles Chaplin.
2 Giovanni Battista Piranesi: Carceri, copperplate engravings, 1750.
3 Ground plan drawing of a British castle in: Louis I. Kahn, *In the Realm of Architecture*. Los Angeles 1991.

Cavern, Sophie Baldassari, p. 56–57

Sophie Baldassari's design also presents a rectangular ground plan with measurements that enter into a dialogue with the waterside and the existing industrial estate. Almost as an antithesis to the vertical landmark of Veiga, this design inserts an enormous, massive plate parallel to the direction of glacial movement along the lake. The great mass actually hovers above the lakeshore. An enormous ring carrier defines the exterior appearance. Within that "enclosure", smaller, standing or suspended volumes create a craggy spatial figure of plateaus, ravines and cave-halls. The "flowing" interior space is clearly segregated from the outside world. The surrounding band of windows between the ring carrier and the quay wall is partitioned by the load-bearing or suspended spatial chamber. This creates a characteristic light for the interior space and frames views out onto the lake.

Sublime interior space, Grégoire Henrioud, p. 58–59

With his design for the shipping yard of the Zürcher Schifffahrtsgesellschaft, Grégoire Henrioud investigated the monumental effect of structure within a gigantic interior space. The hall is dimensioned in a way that allows even the largest ship in the fleet to be accommodated there in the dry dock. The workshop and administrative rooms are organised in the same building, around the hall. Employees enter all areas of the ship using a lateral ramp, while visitors experience the hall from different perspectives. The exhibition spaces of the shipping museum are situated at the front end of the hall and in the spanning girders. The hall itself can also be used for cultural events. The powerful space in the belly of this "supertanker" already indicates a public character through its dimensions.

The atmosphere in the naturally well-lit hall is characterised by the contrast between the immense inner emptiness and the dense, massive surrounding structural elements. This contrast is especially prominent in the fact that the large access ramp is suspended from the ceiling as a massive building element and never touches the ground.

The spatial perception and structural principles reveal analogies with Gothic church buildings and also ships' hulls, weighing tonnes, yet gliding in an apparently weightless way through the water.

Rhythmical space, Allan Cunningham, p. 60–61

Allen Cunningham developed a project for the dance school at the Römerhofplatz in Zurich in which the geometry of the plots, the building physiognomy, the programme and the interior space harmonise in a complex, sophisticated way. The inherent architectural themes of movement and rhythm are explicitly used to give the urban space and also the programmed interior a strong character at this location. The building volume follows the geometry of a curved street, but counteracts this great movement with a series of expressive bays. Inside, this creates a sweeping hall that gains its rhythm through spatial niches and views of the outside world. By contrast, the building's section is a response to the sloping topography of the Römerhofplatz with a gently increasing projecting figure on each floor. That also accommodates the inner organisation with its superposition of the dance rooms, culminating with a large hall on the top floor.

The monumental stairs providing vertical interior access articulate a cascade with selective lateral openings for daylight and views into the urban quarter.

The staged spatial movement and its rhythm climax in the sweeping hall, in which one can easily imagine a connection between space and dancing movement.

Dance hall, Hestia Maillet-Contoz, p. 62–63

Within the sculptural building by Hestia Maillet-Contoz—one could call it a dancing house—a surprisingly calm, albeit no less exciting spatial figure is revealed. Lateral spatial niches are organised around an expansive, tall dance hall. They are limited by enormous supports with integrated stairs. Above it, three small exercise rooms span the space perpendicularly to the hall. Starting at the large hall, places to withdraw develop in this way in niches, stairs and cabinets. Inversely, the smaller, functionally auxiliary rooms produce visual relationship with the "grand stage". The skylights situated between the exercise rooms provide zenithal natural light to the entire spatial layering.

Overall, we see a structured, organised interior world with limited exterior references—a space that fulfils the requirements of choreographic work.

Jérémie Corminboeuf　Structural density
KIBAG Headquarters, Autumn Semester 2013

Left　Sectional view
Right　View into one of the open office areas and first floor plan

51

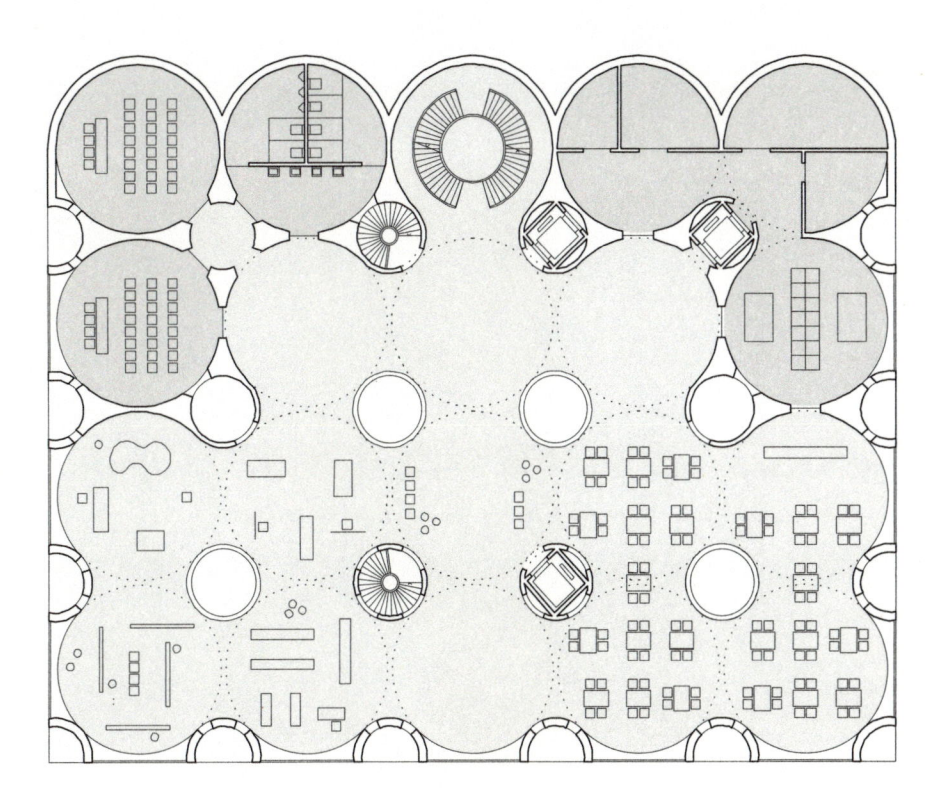

Damien Magat   Spatial machine
                  KIBAG Headquarters, Autumn Semester 2013

Left   Photo of a sectional model and second floor plan
Right   Sectional view

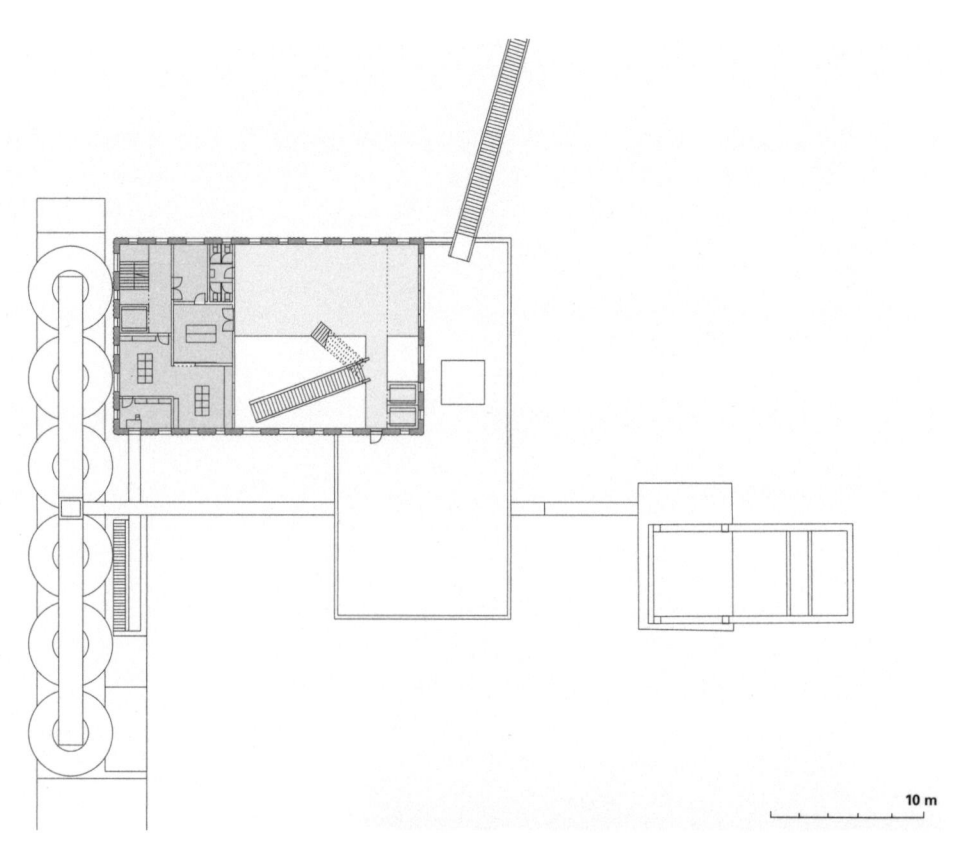

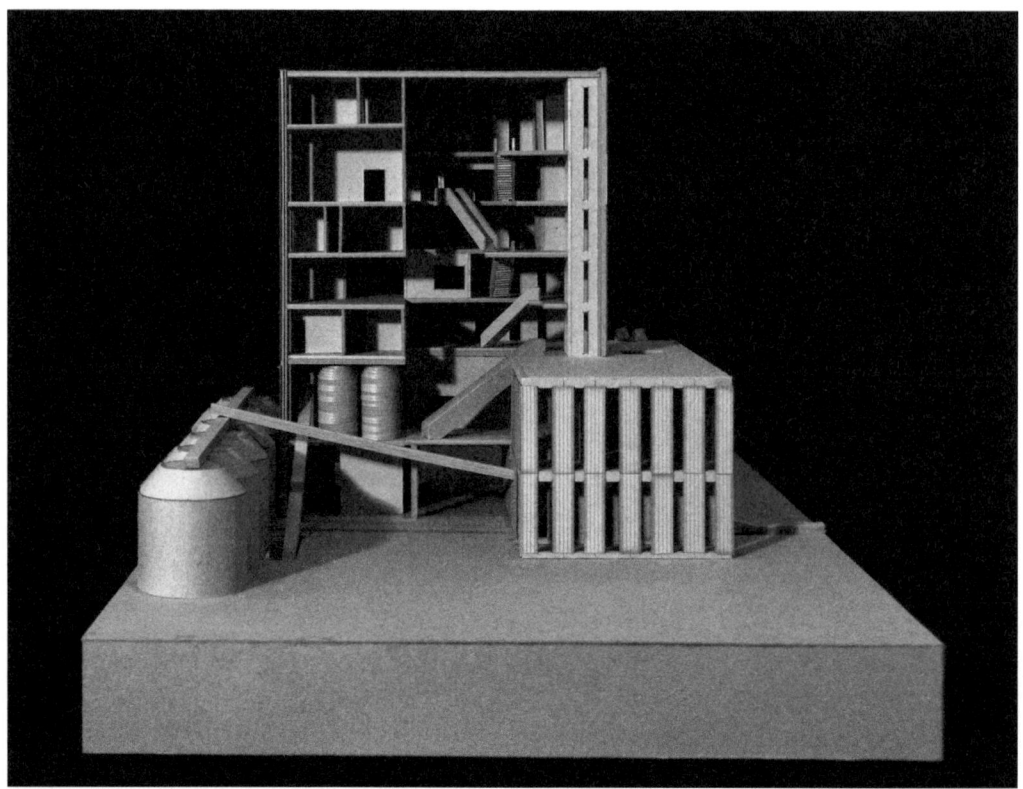

10 m

52

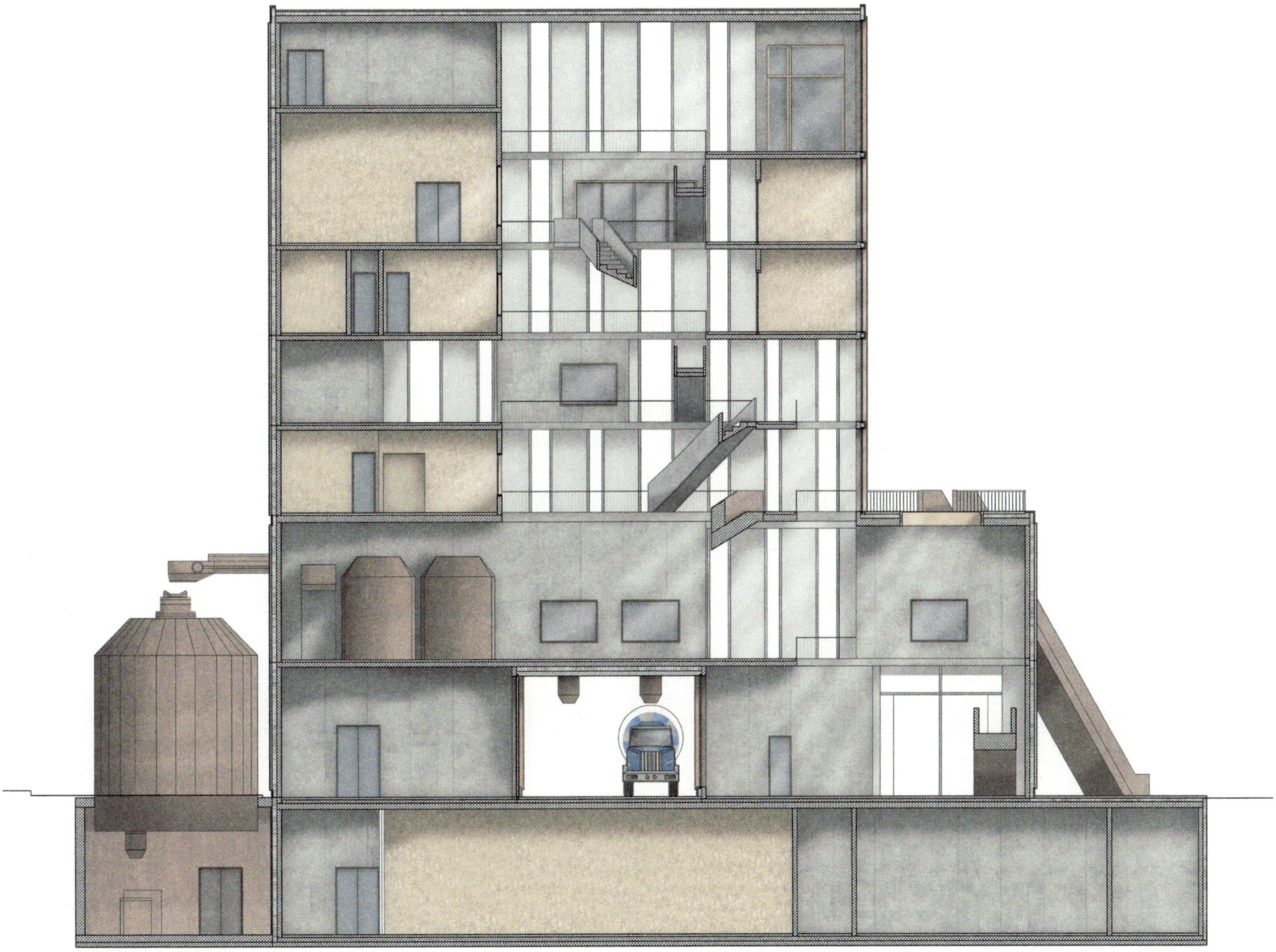

Diogo Veigas	Monolith
	KIBAG Headquarters, Autumn Semester 2013

Left	Sectional view and ground floor plan
Right	Photo of the concept model

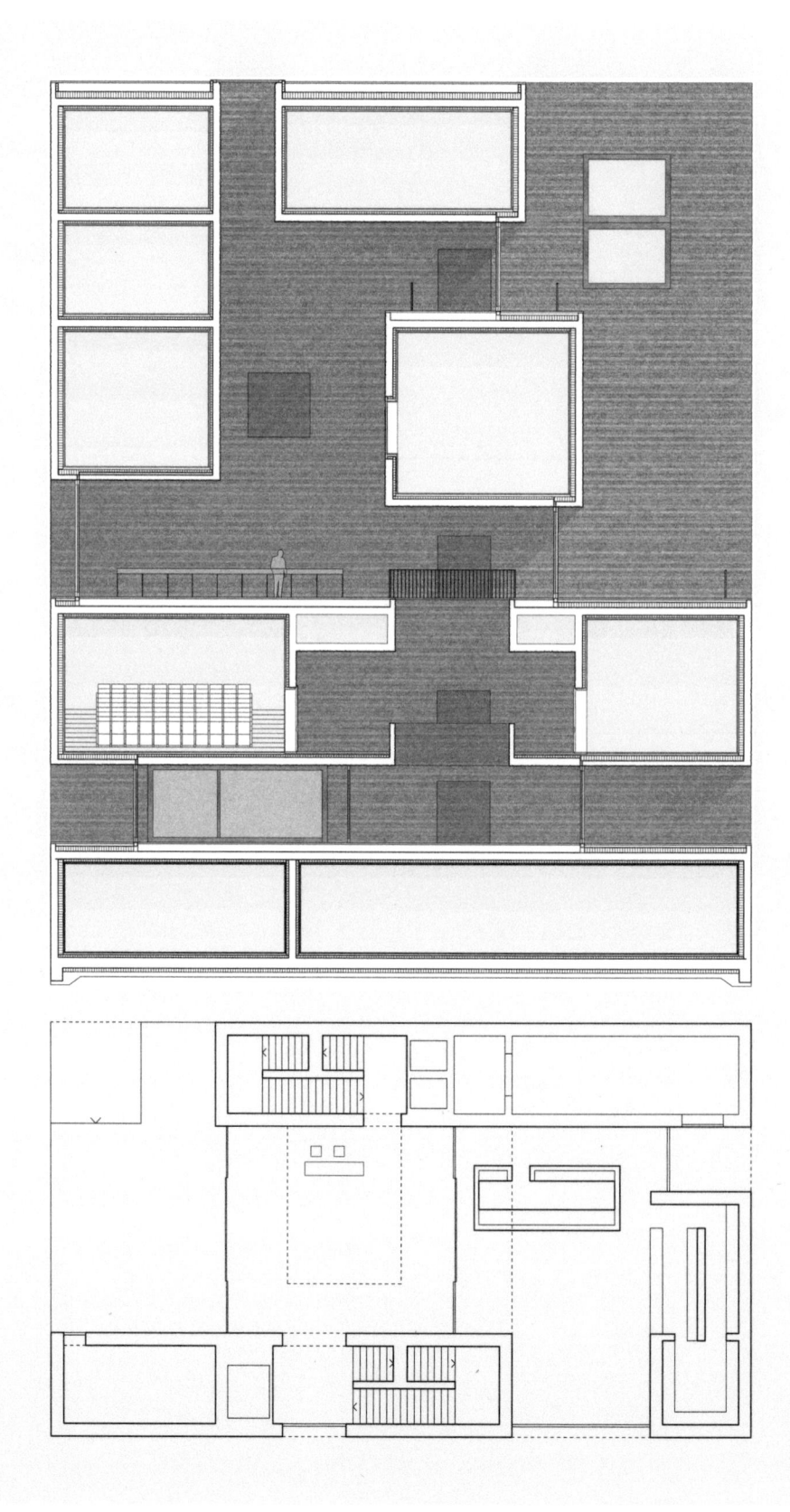

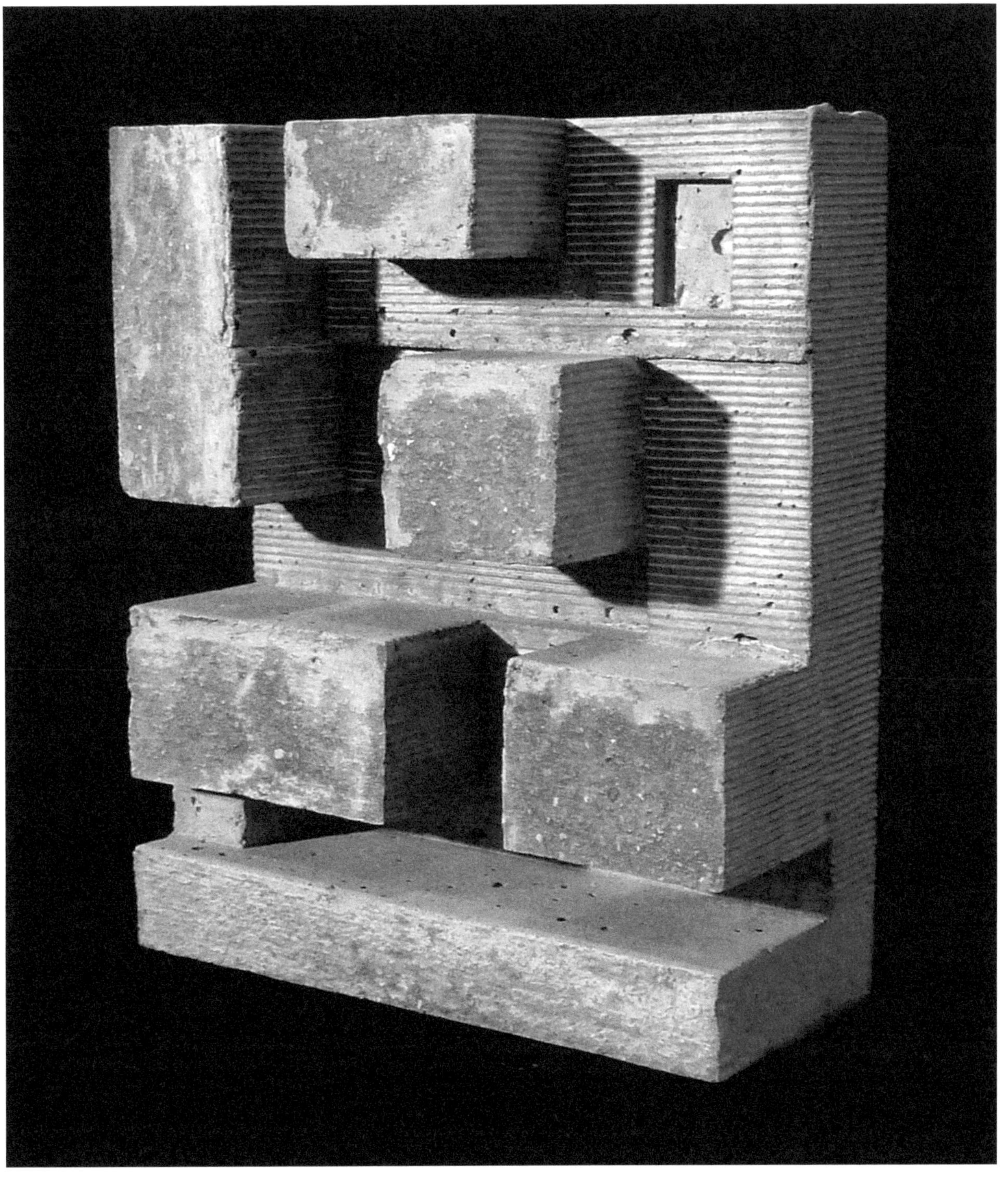

Sophie Baldassari   Cavern
                          KIBAG Headquarters, Autumn Semester 2013

Left   Sectional view and second floor plan
Right   View of the main hall

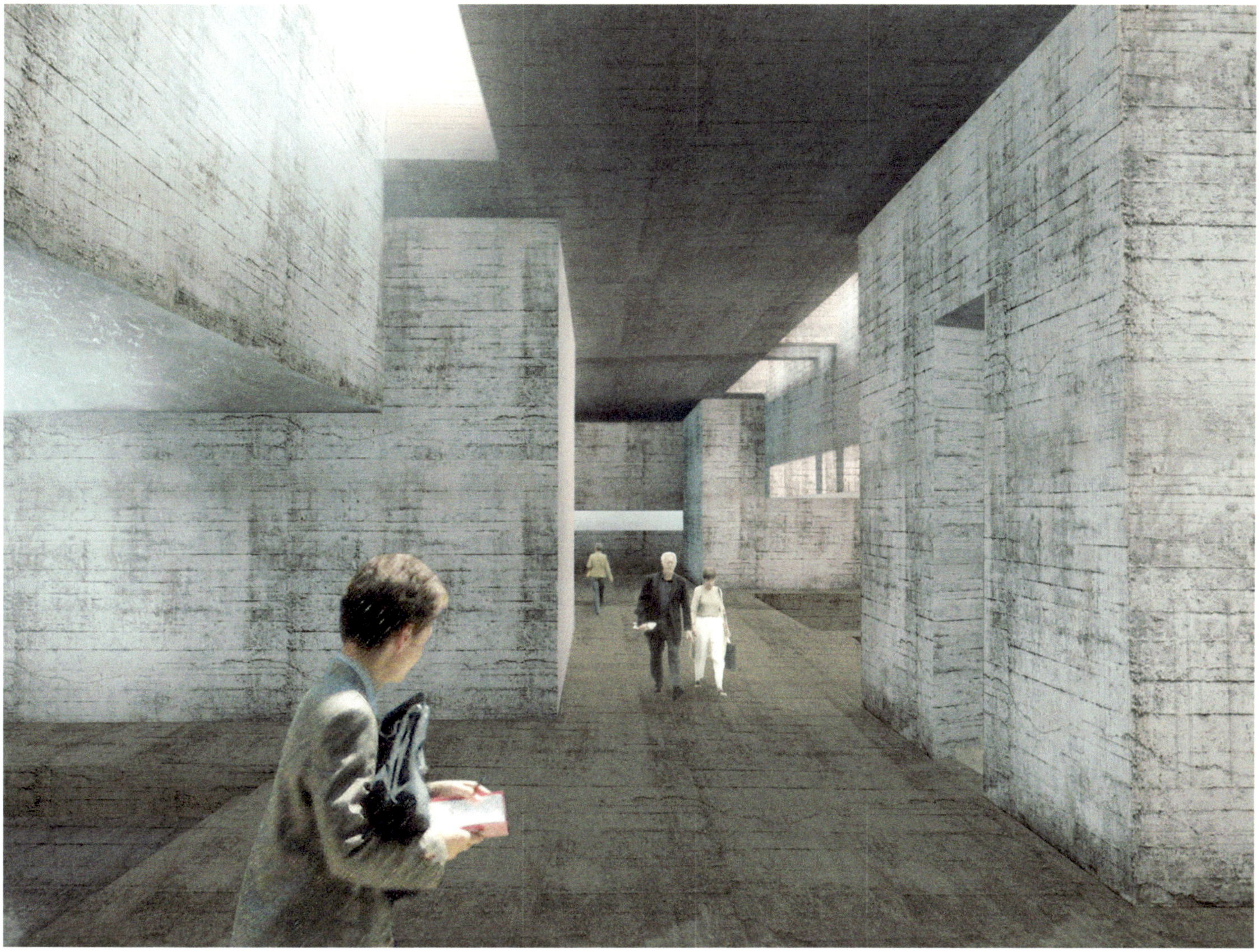

Gregoire Henrioud   Sublime interior space
                    ZSG shipping yard, Autumn Semester 2014

Left   Longitudinal section and ground floor plan
Right   View of the main hall of the shipping yard

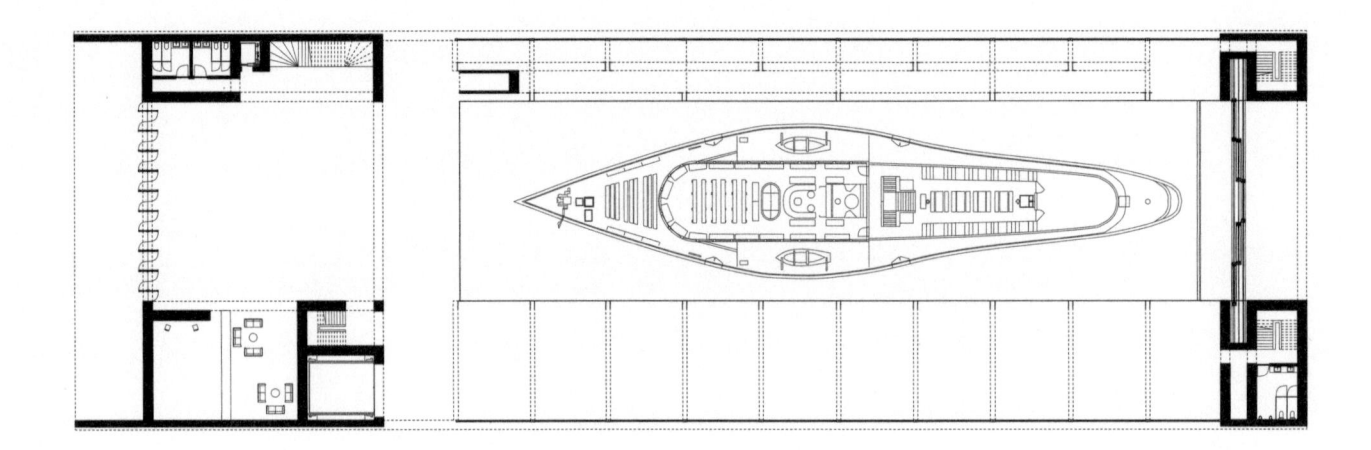

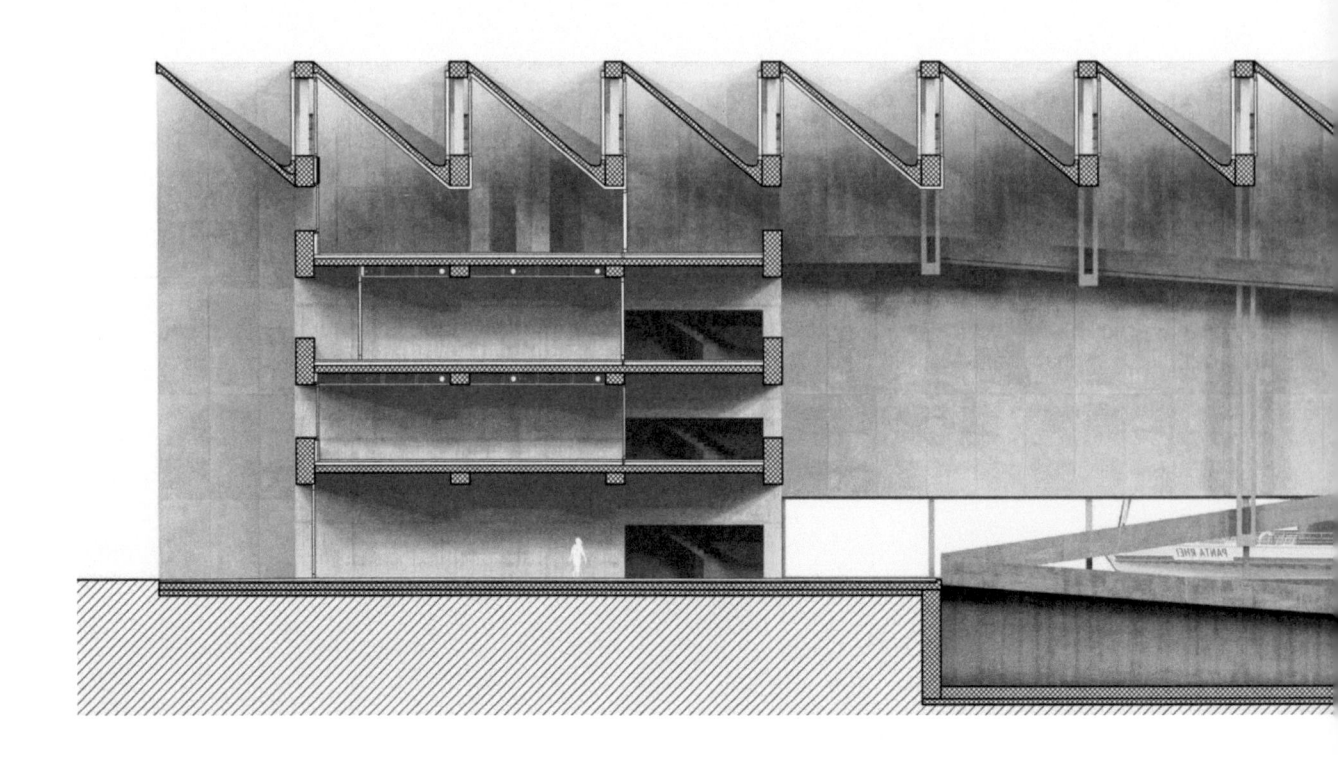

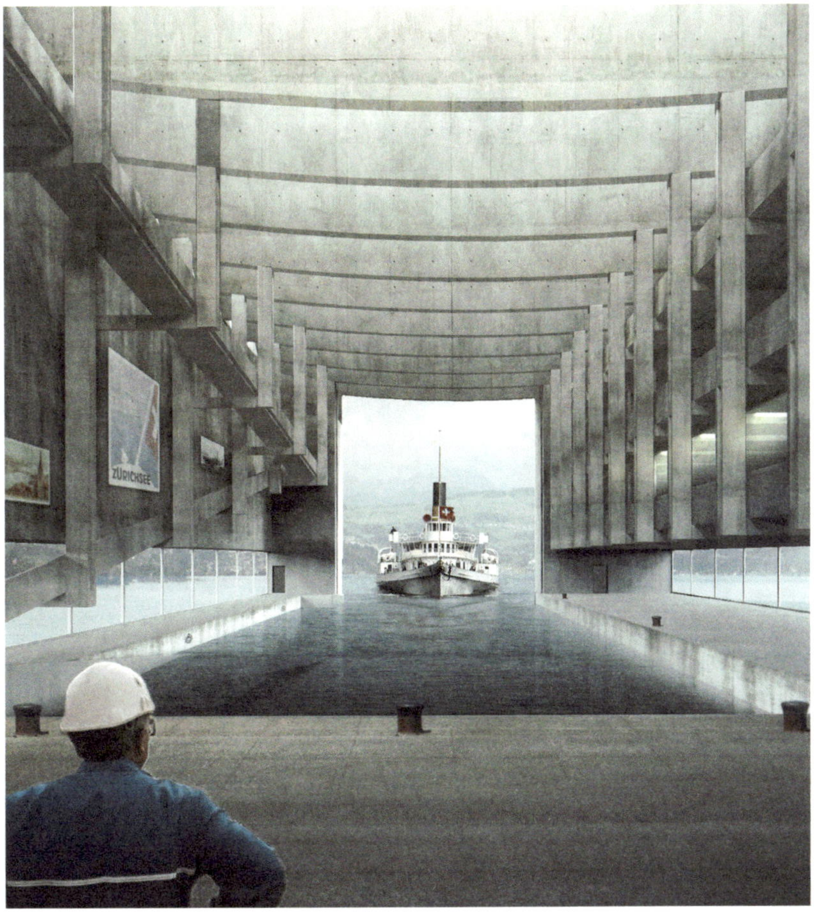
ZÜRICHSEE

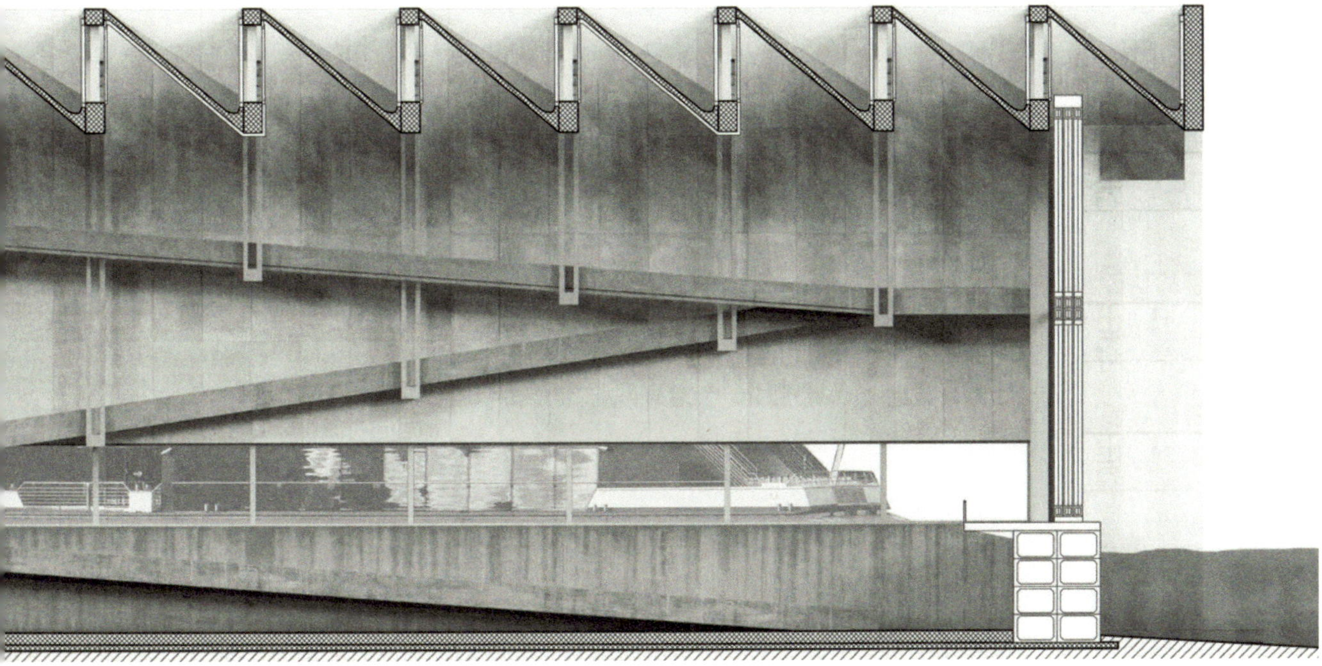

Allan Cunningham Rhythmical space
Dance school on Römerhofplatz, Zurich, Spring Semester 2015

Left   Sectional view
Right View of the dancehall and second floor plan

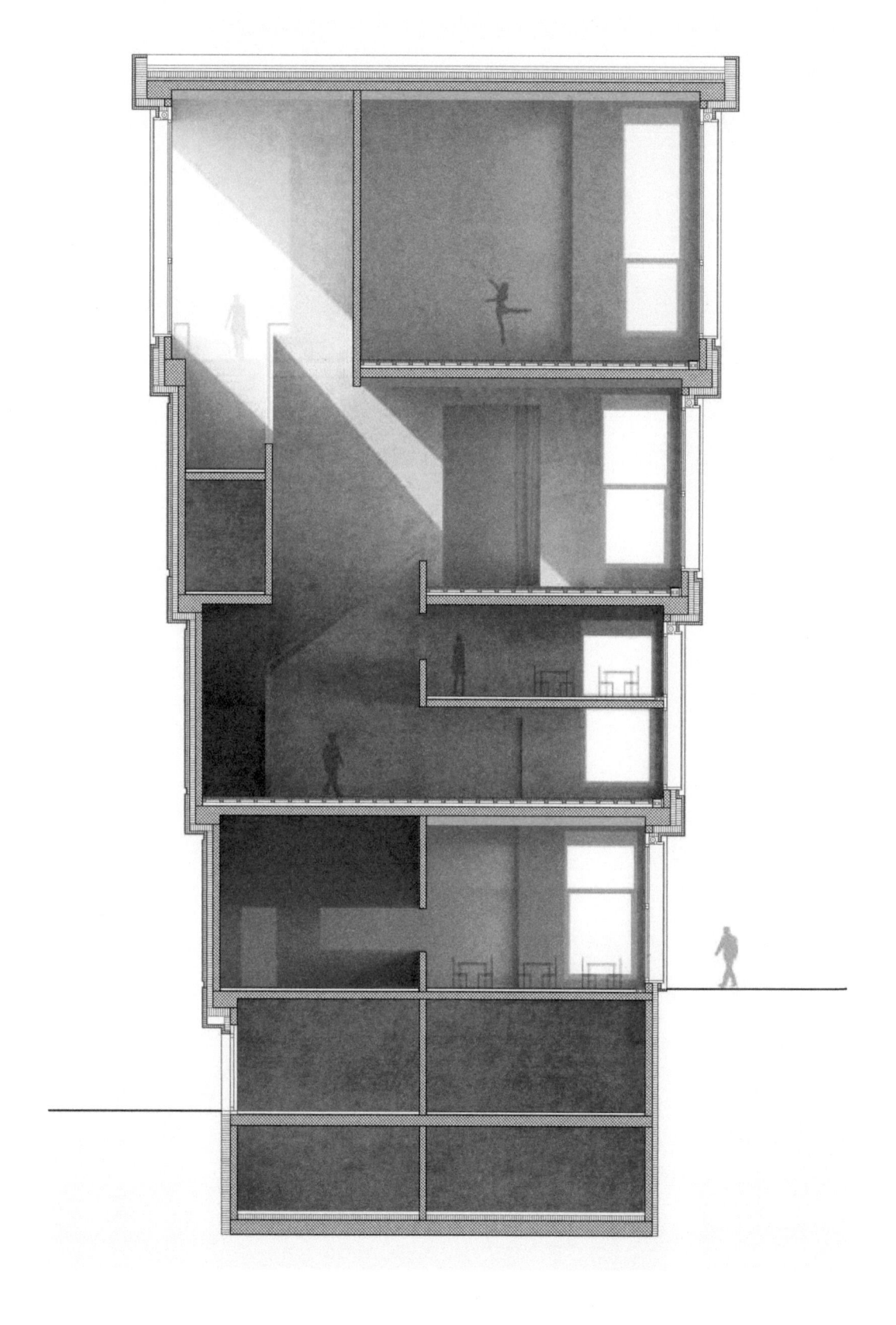

60

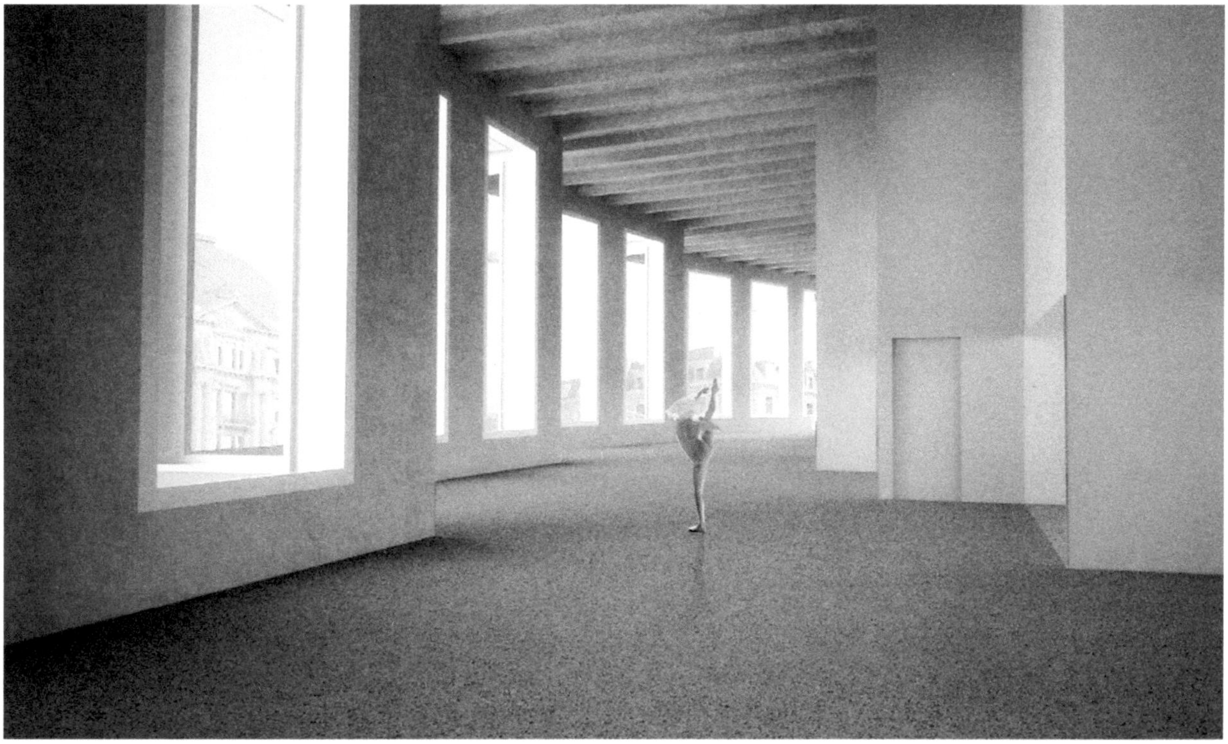

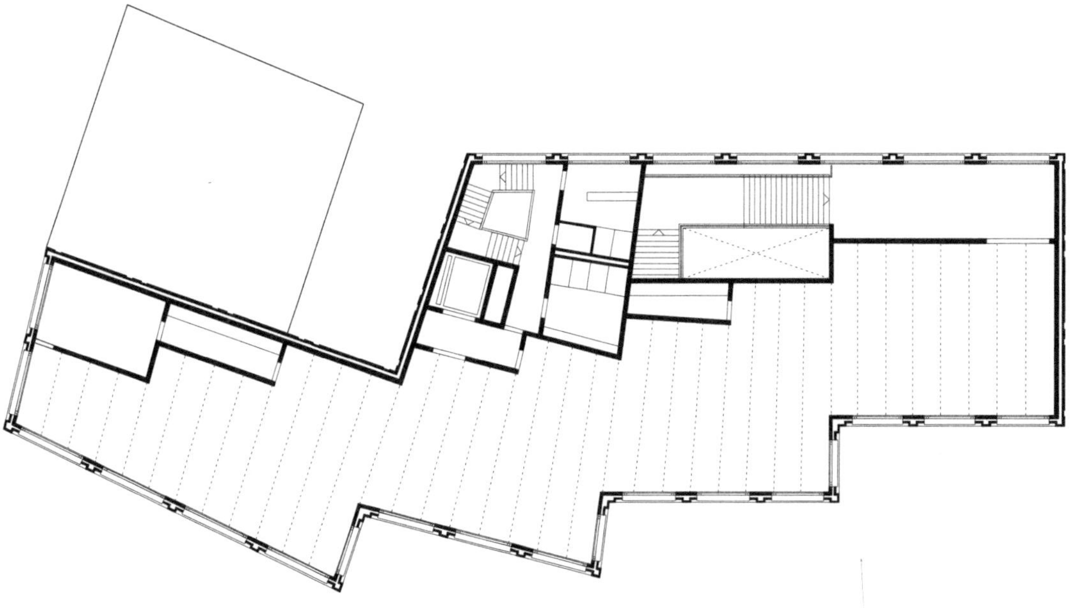

| Hestia Maillet-Contoz | Dance hall
Dance school on Römerhofplatz, Zurich, Spring Semester 2015 |
| --- | --- |
| Left | Longitudinal section and main level floor plan |
| Right | View of the dancehall |

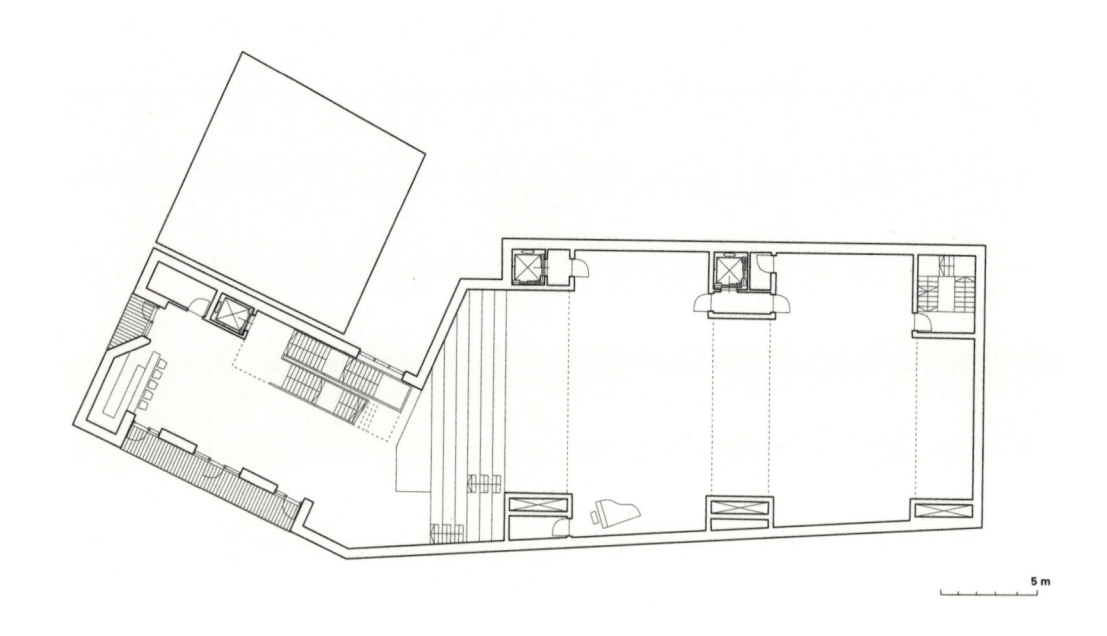

63

Four built spaces

Lorenzo Giuliani, Christian Hönger

Looking at our own work – or more precisely the buildings produced to date by our office – we believe that the following four projects and their respective main spaces come closest to what we would call powerful. The following explanation is based on the three focuses of the supporting structure, spatial figure and voluminosity.

Supporting structure

The two atria and the corridors of the Sihlhof University of Applied Sciences are built in raw fair-faced concrete. The three-dimensional plate structure is almost identical to the spatial formation: everything that defines space is also load-bearing. No difference is made between areas supporting greater or lesser loads and the transition between them is smooth. The supporting structure is formworked in a sophisticated way while remaining raw, thereby creating a deliberate archaic quality for the material and allowing the college's common rooms and atria to be experienced both as walkable, public spaces and as part of the load-bearing structure.

In the case of the St. Gallen University of Applied Sciences, the load-bearing structure of the building envelope is mounted onto a system of supports and plates with a strict 2.5-metre support grid. The raw load-bearing structure is visible in all workrooms, the library area and the entrance hall. For the sake of spatial perception, the logic of the supporting structure is deliberately suspended: in the library area, the visibility on the tower side is limited, where there is continuity towards the exterior tower façade, while the other three sides contrast with apparently hovering reading galleries, as the load-bearing structure is transferred to the book towers. In this case, the load-bearing structure appears to be symbolic, since the books, stores of knowledge, seem to support the reading galleries. The entrance hall is handled in a similar way, since the load-bearing structure on the tower side faces the opposite load-bearing walls of the public areas.

The new steel supporting structure of the vonRoll lecture theatre building is literally swallowed by the insulating wooden element walls. By contrast, the existing timber supports and the delicate roof framework are highlighted by shifting the location of the new wall system with respect to the existing structure, thereby appearing to be non-supporting. The principle is explicitly recognisable in the side foyer, where the existing support stands freely beneath the overhang in the foyer and above it in the large lecture theatre.

In the Hilti Innovation Centre, the level of peripheral uses is supported using a simple support/plate structure to achieve a high level of flexibility. By contrast, the testing hall is covered without any supports. At first glance, the large distance seems to be entirely bridged by the hovering, materially homogenous bridges. The spatial trusses are only recognisable in fragments and indirectly through the windows of the bridges. One can sense the supporting structure in the hall without it being visible.

Spatial figure

In the case of the Sihlhof University of Applied Sciences, the staggered building volume with a polygonal ground plan, a spatial figure with two offset atria, is shifted in a sculptural way, as is recognisable in the models and sectional plans. On every second floor, this figure interlocks with the corridors and structurally penetrates the surrounding building envelope in three places.

The two atria of the St. Gallen University of Applied Sciences are spacers between the ring-like building plinth and the embedded tower. While the multistorey library interlocks with the corridors of the teaching level, the exterior courtyard achieves a spatial continuity in the ground-level entrance hall, which acts as a covered urban space that makes it possible to perceive the full height of the tower structure.

For the vonRoll lecture theatre building, an articulated spatial figure between the sculpturally formed lecture theatres and the historical building envelop of the original switch construction hall becomes an interior urban space serving as a foyer. Large windows that dissolve the framed nature of the lecture theatres as black boxes connect the foyer and lecture theatres in a spatially comprehensive way.

The long testing hall inside the Hilti Innovation Centre forms a spatial figure that expands by one floor in the public areas, opening structurally towards the south and over six atria towards the zenithal light. The testing hall forms the centre of the interaction between workshops, laboratories and office landscapes. The acoustic disconnection enables visual interaction between strongly differing uses. From the testing hall, which is subjected to considerable noise emissions, it is possible to look into all areas, for instance the cosy common rooms on the bridges and vice versa.

Voluminosity

The Sihlhof University of Applied Sciences uses voluminosity to create the impression of a heavy mass, whereas the spans evoke tangible relief while walking through the atria and the entrance hall, even creating the impression of lightness. The voluminosity and variety of the spatial figure invoke highly contrasting feelings. The all-over character of the material, combined with the inner verticality and complexity of the space, can irritate one's sense of balance and inspire a sense of weightlessness.

In the library space of the St. Gallen University of Applied Sciences, the wooden trusses are aligned in a flush way with the supporting structure, uniting them in a single surface and highlighting the voluminosity of the spatial form. The hovering library galleries and the projection over the southern courtyard undermine the otherwise consistent logic of the load-bearing elements in favour of the spatial effects of heaviness and lightness.

In the case of the vonRoll lecture theatre building, the outside of the inserted lecture theatre bodies and the inside of the lecture theatres themselves are clad in a shell of thin boards. The voluminous joints of the cladding boards and the detailed finishing cover up the lack of material strength. The character of the foyer as an inner exterior space is enhanced through the untreated outer shell, which shows traces of its use, as a special "in-between" place that is climatically experienced as merely a tempered intermediary space.

For noise-insulation reasons, the testing hall of the Hilti Innovation Centre was completely clad in oscillating, reinforced acoustic plates. The voluminous joints of the wall, bridge and underside rejects their expression as cladding and suggests a homogenous silver-grey space.

Giuliani Hönger — Sihlhof University of Applied Sciences, Zurich, 2000–2003

Left — Sectional view of the two atria and first floor plan
Right — View of the upper atrium

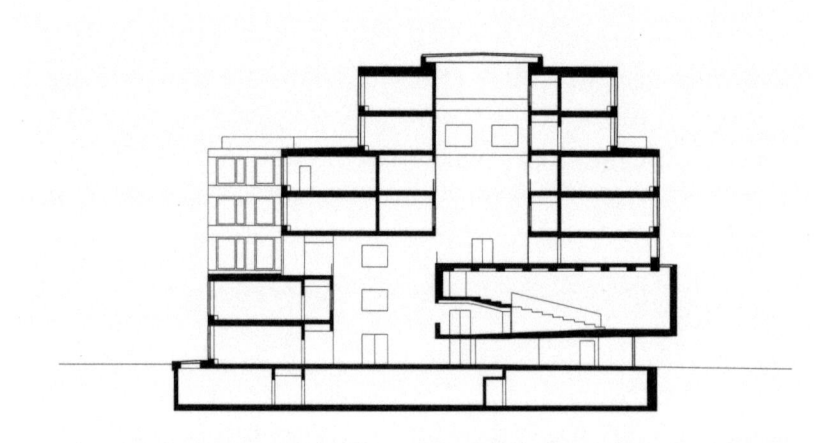

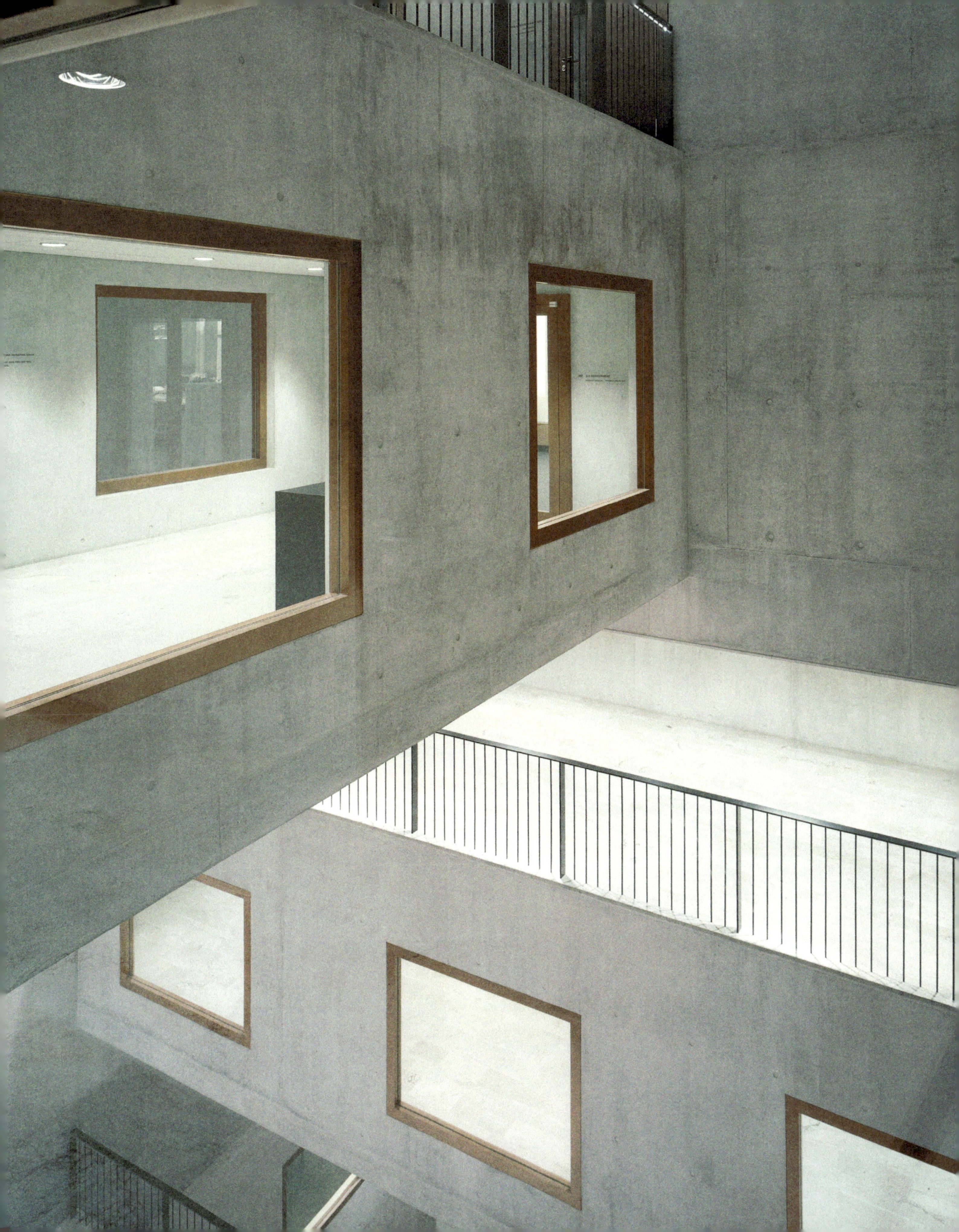

Giuliani Hönger St. Gallen University of Applied Sciences, 2003–2013

Left Sectional view of the library and entrance lobby, first floor plan

Right View of the library atrium

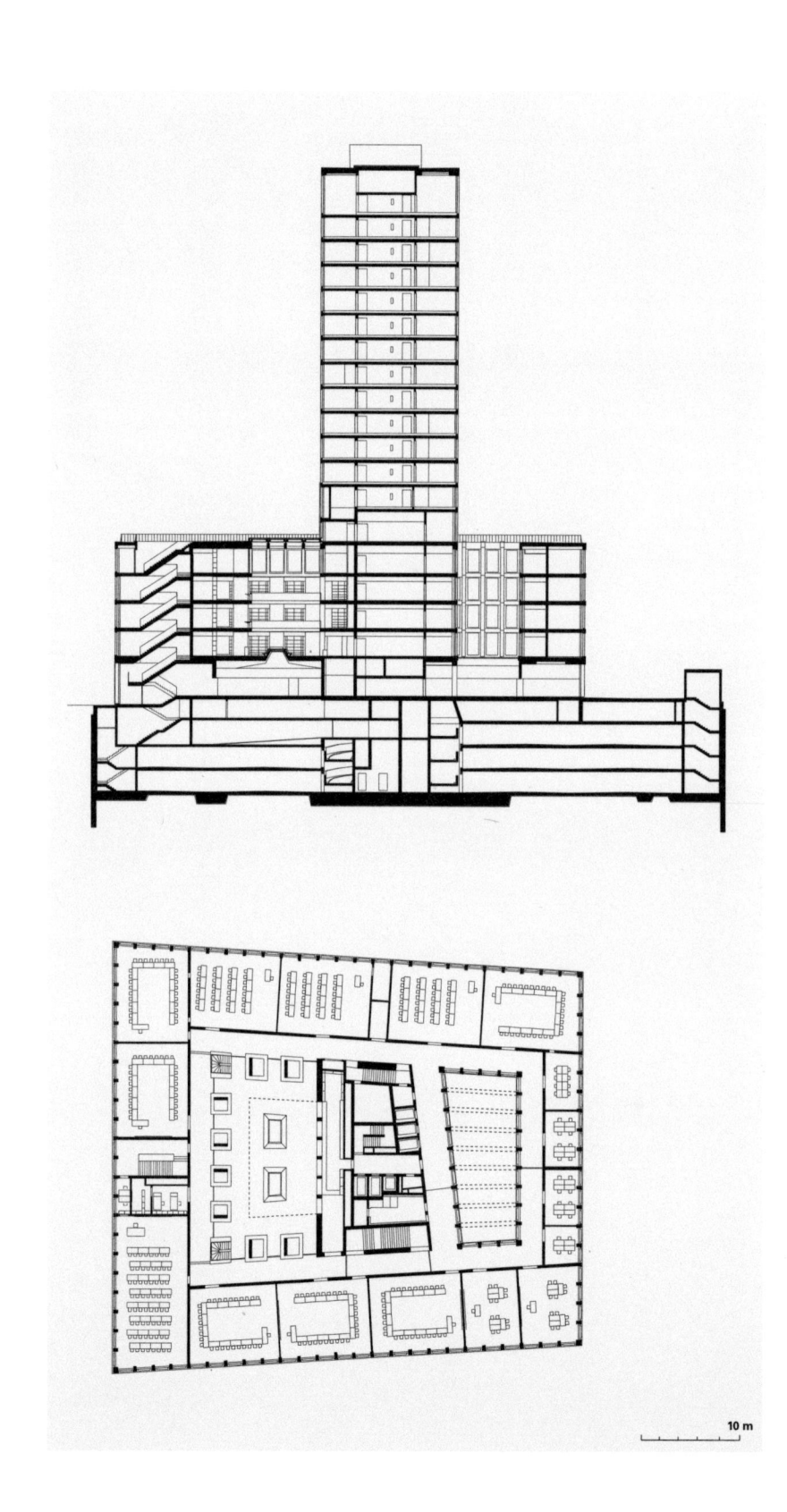

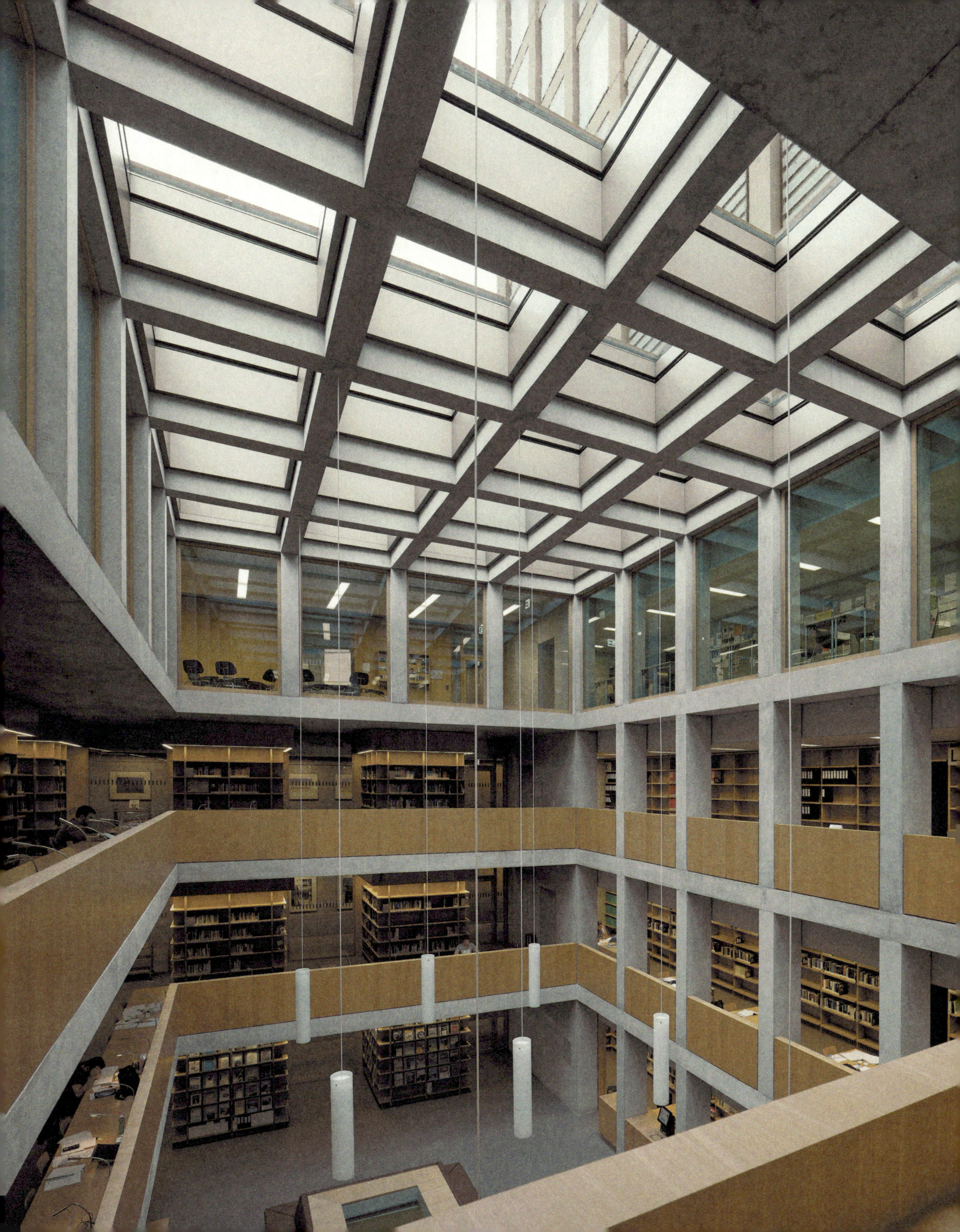

Giuliani Hönger — Lecture theatre building, vonRoll Areal, Bern, 2005–2010

Left — Sectional view of the hall and ground floor plan
Right — View of the hall between the existing structures and the integrated lecture theatres

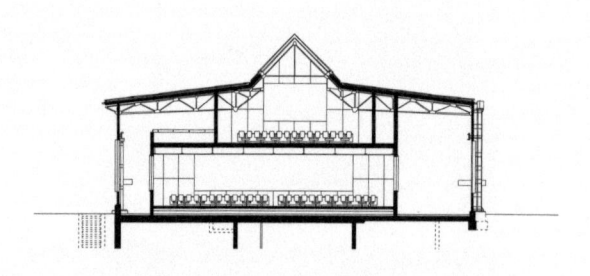

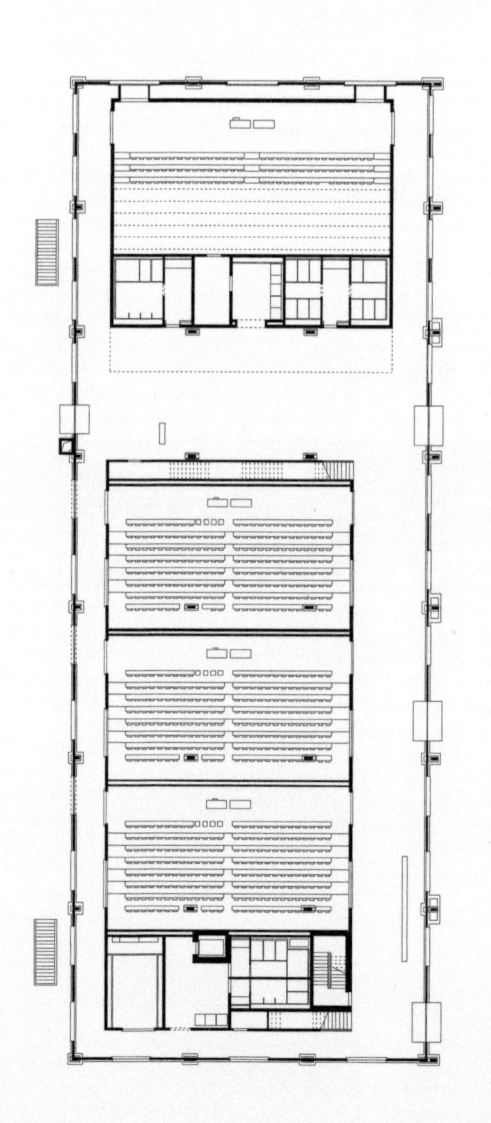

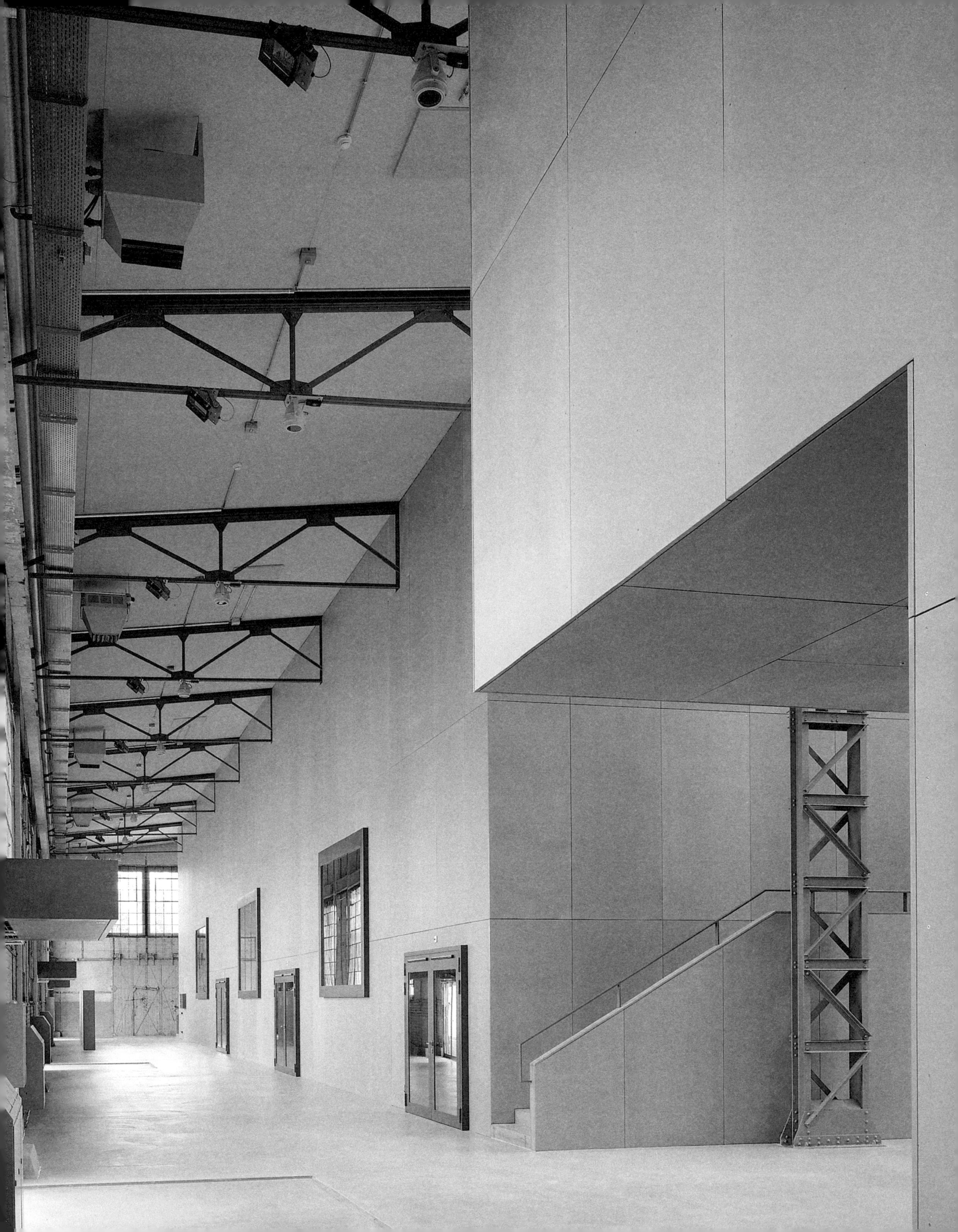

Giuliani Hönger   Hilti Innovation Centre, Schaan, 2005–2010

Left   Longitudinal section of the testing hall
        and third floor plan
Right   View of the testing hall

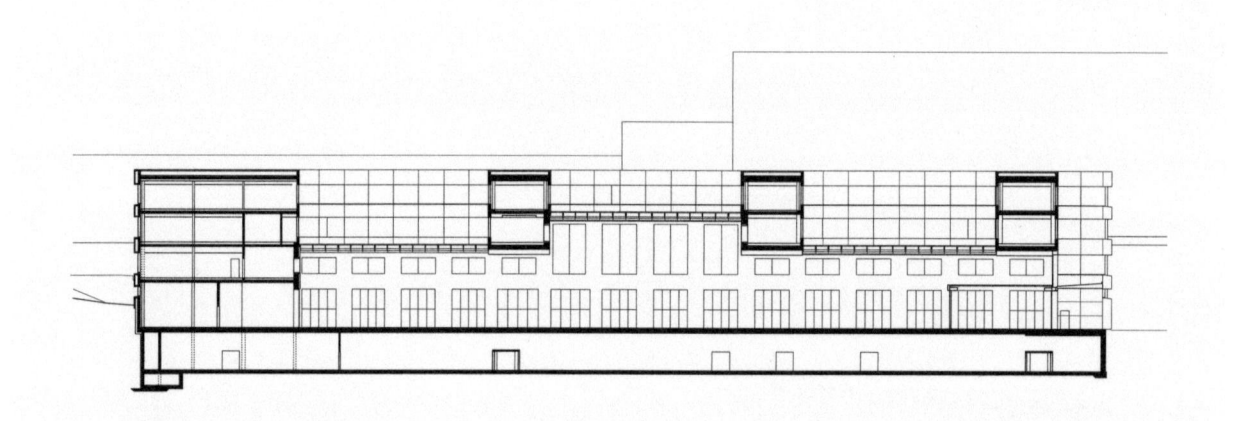

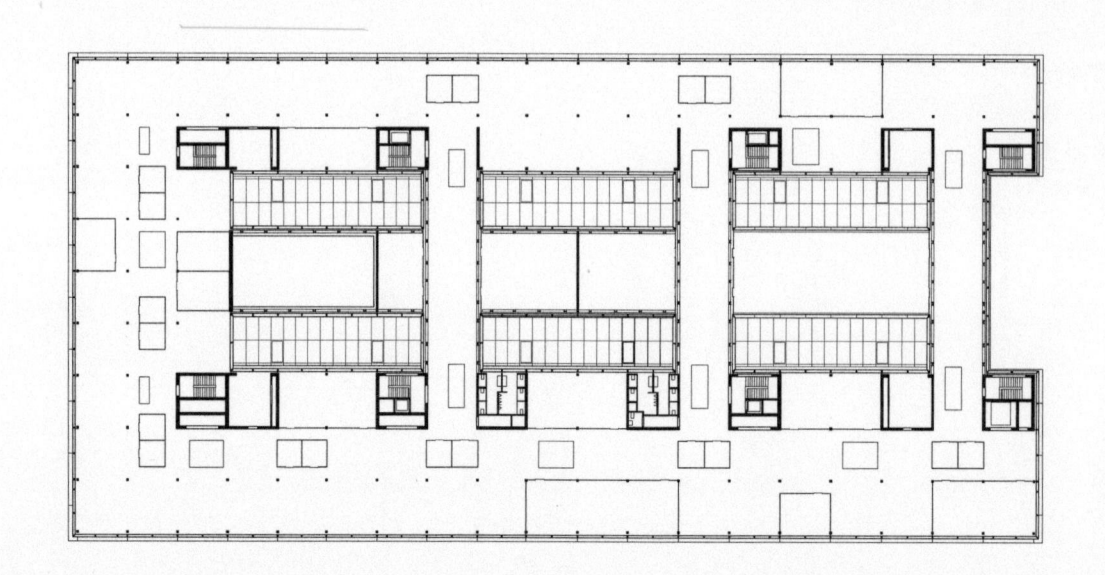

10 m

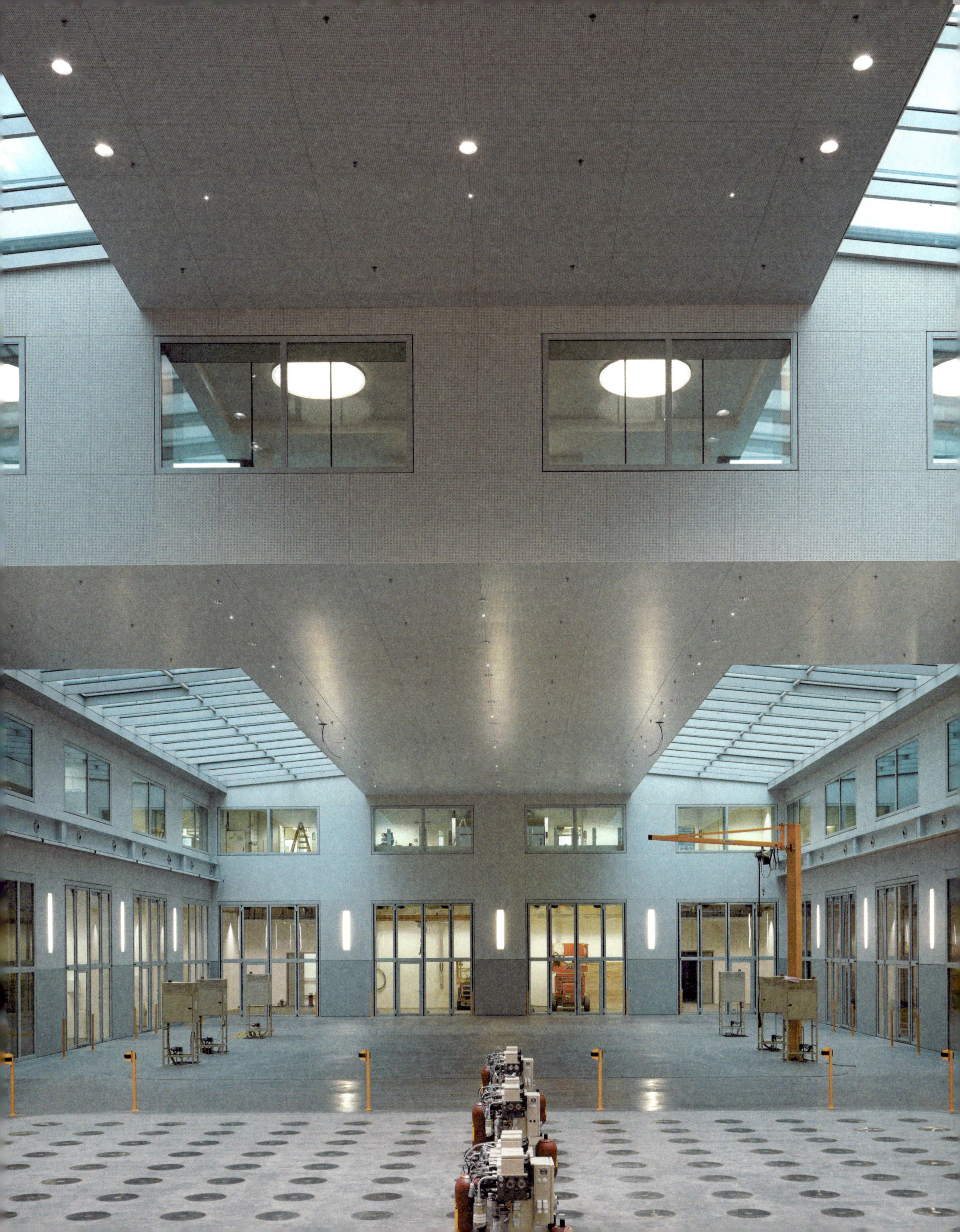

Project facts

Sihlhof University of Applied Sciences, Zurich

Contract	Invitation project competition, 1999, 1st Prize
Planning and construction	2000–2008
Employees	Lorenzo Giuliani, Christian Hönger, Marcel Santer (Project Manager) Andreas Derrer, Nilufar Kahnemouyi, Adrian Langhart, Roger Naegeli, Tibor Pataky, Rico Wasescha
Building management	Bosshard+Partner, Zurich
Structural engineer	Dr. Lüchinger+Meyer Bauingenieure, ZH
Building technology planning	Haerter & Partner, Zurich Schwengeler enercon, Winterthur ETA, Glarus

St. Gallen University of Applied Sciences

Contract	Open project competition, 2003, 1st Prize
Planning and construction	2003–2013
Employees	Lorenzo Giuliani, Christian Hönger, Bianca Hohl (Project Manager), Tobias Greiner (Project Manager, finishing from 2010), Marco Fitze, Prisca Lieberherr, Patrick Peter, Andrea Stehlin, Christian Senn, Alexandra Weis, Samuel Sutter;
Project stage Pre-/Building project	Marcel Santer (Project Manager), Sabine Annen, Daniel Gardi, Monique Jüttner, Martin Puppel, Regula Steinmann, Daniel Vega, Sigrid Wittl
Building management	b+p Baurealisation, Zurich
Structural engineer	Dr. Lüchinger+Meyer Bauingenieure, ZH
Building technology planning	3-Plan, Winterthur (HVAC, coordination) mtp, Uster (electrics) Tri Air, Jona (plumbing, sprinklers) Boxler MSRL-Engineering, Rapperswil-Jona (MSRL)

Lecture theatre building, vonRoll Areal, Bern

Contract	Open European competition, 2004, 1st Prize
Planning and construction	2005–2010
Employees	Lorenzo Giuliani, Christian Hönger, Julia Koch (Project Manager from 2008), Gabriele Oesterle (Project Manager until 2008), Bianca Hohl, Caroline Schönauer
Building management	b+p Baurealisation, Zurich
Structural engineer	Dr. Joseph Schwartz Consulting, Zug
Timber structural engineer	Walter Bieler AG, Bonaduz
Building technology planning	Amstein+Walthert, Bern

Hilti Innovation Centre, Schaan

Contract	Invitation competition (2 stages), 2008, 1st Prize
Planning and construction	2008–2014
Employees	Lorenzo Giuliani, Christian Hönger, Martin Künzler (Project Manager from 2010), Thomas Hochstrasser (Project Manager until 2009), Matthias Bircher, Reto Bleiker, Isabelle Bucher, Ivo Bürgin, Marcus Hartmann, Roger Heeb, Sander Lückers, Christian Maag, Kristina Mueller, Monika Sailer, Silvia Schneider, Lukas Sonderegger, Tobias Ziegler
Building management	Caretta+Weidmann Baumanagement, ZH
Structural engineer	Dr. Schwarz Consulting, Zug Wenaweser+Partner Bauingenieure, Schaan
Building technology planning	Sytek AG, Binningen (coordination, electrics) Aicher, De Martin, Zweng AG, Zürich (ventilation, cooling, air conditioning) tib Technik im Bau AG, Luzern (plumbing)

About the authors

Raphael Dunant studied at the ETH Zurich. After graduating in 2009, he worked in various architectural offices, including for Christian Penzel in Zurich and Graber Pulver Architekten. From 2014 to 2015 he was Assistant at the EPFL to the Giuliani Hönger Guest Professorship. In 2015 he founded DUNANT Architecte EPFZ in Geneva. He is currently Assistant to the Guest Professors Graber Pulver at the EPFL and working on his own research project with the photographer Leo Fabrizio, studying the work of Fernand Pouillon: *Rediscovering Fernand Pouillon*.

Lorenzo Giuliani studied Architecture at the ETH Zurich, where he worked as an Assistant to several Professors after graduating. 25 years ago, he founded the architectural office Giuliani Hönger in Zurich together with Christian Hönger. In parallel with his office work, he was a Lecturer in Architecture and Urban Planning Analysis and Professor of Design and Construction at the ZHAW Winterthur. From 2013 to 2015, he held a joint Guest Professorship with Christian Hönger at the EPFL. The main themes of the learning content were *Powerful Spaces* and *Urban Constellation*.

Christian Hönger studied Architecture at the ETH Zurich, where he worked as an Assistant to several Professors after graduating. 25 years ago, he founded the architectural office Giuliani Hönger in Zurich together with Lorenzo Giuliani. In parallel with his office work, he was a Lecturer at the FHNW Muttenz and Professor of Design and Construction at the HSLU Lucerne, where he also conducted research. From 2013 to 2015, he held a joint Guest Professorship with Lorenzo Giuliani at the EPFL. The main themes of the learning content were *Powerful Spaces* and *Urban Constellation*.

Michael Meier studied Architecture at the ETH Zurich. After graduating in 2008, he worked in the architectural office Jessenvollenweider in Basel. As a Project Manager, he managed competitions until 2012 and worked in parallel on implementing various projects. From 2012 to 2014, he taught at the ETH Lausanne in the team of the Giuliani Hönger Guest Professorship. Since 2012 he has been an independent architect and leads the architectural office saas sàrl, Geneva together with Guillaume Yersin.

Tibor Pataky studied Architecture at the RWTH Aachen and the IUAV in Venice, after which he worked in various architectural offices, including Giuliani Hönger and Diener & Diener. He was subsequently Assistant to the Guest Lecturers Caruso St John and Markus Peter at the ETH Zurich. He is currently Assistant to Christophe van Gerrewey, Tenure Track Assistant Professor of Architectural Theory (Laboratoire ACHT) at the EPF Lausanne and is working on a dissertation on the early work of OMA / Rem Koolhaas. He is also the author of the novel *Fruchtmann*, which was published in 2015.

Joseph Schwartz has been Full Professor of Structural Design at the ETH Zurich since February 2008. He studied and attained his doctorate in the Department of Civil Engineering at the ETH Zurich. Between 2001 and 2008, he was Lecturer at the Fachhochschule Zentralschweiz. He is co-author of the books *Bemessung von Betontragwerken mit Spannungsfeldern* (1996) and *Mauerwerk* (1998), *Before Steel* (2010) and *Holz: Stoff oder Form* (2014). Since 2002 he has led his own engineering office based in Zug and works closely together with several leading Swiss architects.

Selected Bibliography

Sihlhof University of Applied Sciences, Zurich

giuliani.hönger Architekten: *Schnittwerk. Eine Ausstellung von giuliani.hönger Architekten im Architekturforum Aedes, Berlin, 22. Januar bis 4. März 2010.* Zurich 2010, p. 30–37.

Axel Simon, "Hoflandschaft am Hauptbahnhof", in: *Velux Tageslicht Award.* Supplement to *Hochparterre* Nr. 3, 2010, p. 14–15.

Tobias Schwarzer (Ed.), *best architects 09.* Düsseldorf 2008, p. 142–145.

Jacques Lucan, *Matières 9. L'espace architectural. Hypothèse pour une spatialité texturée.* Lausanne 2008, p. 6–17.

ETH Zurich–gta (Ed.), *giuliani. hönger. dreidimensional.* Zurich 2006, p. 38–47.

Andrea Deplazes, *Architektur konstruieren. Vom Rohmaterial zum Bauwerk.* Basel 2008. p. 283, 384–394.

Axel Simon, "Beyond the Swiss box", in: *A10–New European architecture*, No. 3, 2005, p. 58–60.

Arthur Rüegg / Reto Gadola / Daniel Spillmann / Michael Widrig, *Die Unschuld des Betons. Wege zu einer materialspezifischen Architektur.* Zurich 2004 p. 20–21.

Christian Holl, "Vom Reiz der Zwänge. Fachhochschule Sihlhof, Zürich". In: *db – Deutsche Bauzeitung* No. 71, 2004, p. 38–48.

Matthias Ackermann, "Konturen. Neubau der Fachhochschule Sihlhof, von giuliani.hönger, Zürich", in: *Werk, Bauen + Wohnen* No. 7 / 8, 2003, p. 22–31.

Judit Solt, "Komplexe Verschränkungen", in: *Archithese* No. 3, 2003, p. 72–77.

Roderik Hönig, *Fachhochschule Sihlhof. Architektur des neuen Selbstbewusstseins.* Supplement to *Hochparterre* No. 6 / 7, 2003.

St. Gallen University of Applied Sciences

Docu Media Schweiz (Ed.), *2016 Schweizer Baudokumentation.* Rüschlikon 2016, B26.

Tibor Joanelly, "Gerüst und Gefüge. Neubau Fachhochschulzentrum St.Gallen von Giuliani Hönger", in: *Werk, Bauen + Wohnen* No. 9, 2013, p. 12–19.

Roland Brunner / Denis Pflug, "Bibliothek der Fachhochschule, St. Gallen", in: *Lignum Holzbulletin, Innenräume* No. 108, 2013, p. 2380–2385.

giuliani.hönger Architekten, *Schnittwerk. Eine Ausstellung von giuliani. hönger Architekten im Architekturforum Aedes, Berlin, 22. Januar bis 4. März 2010.* Zurich 2010, p. 48–55.

Andrea Deplazes, *Architektur konstruieren. Vom Rohmaterial zum Bauwerk.* Basel 2008.

ETH Zurich–gta (Ed.): *giuliani. hönger. dreidimensional.* Zürich 2006, p. 104–111.

Ina Schmid, "Fachhochschule Bahnhof Nord, St. Gallen" in: *Hochparterre Wettbewerbe* No. 2, 2003, p. 37–49.

Weichenbauhalle lecture theatre building, Bern

Jean-Daniel Gross, "Fabrikstrasse 6. Hörsaalgebäude des Hochschulzentrums vonRoll, ehemals Weichenbauhalle der vonRoll AG, 1914, Architekt unbekannt", in: *Denkmalpflege in der Stadt Bern.* Bern 2013, p. 163–168.

Sibylle Kramer, *Rough Interiors.* Salenstein 2013, p. 34–37

Katharina Marchal, "Die verwandelte Halle. Hörsaalgebäude in der Weichenbauhalle, Bern", in: *Modulor* No. 5, 2011, p. 64–70

Holger Wallbaum / Susanne Kytzia / Samuel Kellenberger, *Nachhaltig bauen. Lebenszyklus, Systeme, Szenarien, Verantwortung.* Zurich 2011, p. 124–139.

Tobias Schwarzer (Ed.), *best architects 11.* Düsseldorf 2010, p. 194–197.

Caspar Schärer, "Innerer Städtebau. Hörsaalzentrum in der Weichenbauhalle auf dem vonRoll-Areal in Bern von Giuliani Hönger Architekten", in: *Werk, Bauen + Wohnen* No. 11, 2010, p. 14–19

giuliani.hönger Architekten, *Schnittwerk. Eine Ausstellung von giuliani.hönger Architekten im Architekturforum Aedes, Berlin, 22. Januar bis 4. März 2010.* Zurich 2010, p. 38–47.

ETH Zurich–gta (Ed.): *giuliani. hönger. dreidimensional.* Zurich 2006, p. 52–55.

Hilti Innovation Centre, Schaan

Tibor Joanelly, "Kopf und Hand. Das Innovationszentrum von Hilti in Schaan von Giuliani Hönger Architekten", in: *Werk, Bauen + Wohnen* No. 4, 2016, p. 10–17.

Wilhelm Bauer / Jörg Kelter, "Vom Konzept in die Realität. Eine agile multifunktionale Arbeitswelt entsteht", in: *Werk, Bauen + Wohnen* No. 4, 2016, p. 18–19.

Docu Media Schweiz (Ed.), 2016 Schweizer Baudokumentation. Rüschlikon 2016, B08.

Burkhard Fröhlich, "Balthasar Neumann Preis 2016. Auszeichnung. Hilti Innovation Center, Schaan/LIE", in: *DBZ–Deutsche Bauzeitschrift* No. 4, 2016, p. 18–19.

Docu Media Schweiz (Ed.), "Arc-Award. Kategorie Arbeitswelten. 1. Rang. Hilti Innovations-Zentrum", in: *Viso, Sonderausgabe* 2015, p. 16–21.

Tobias Schwarzer (Ed.), *best architects 16.* Düsseldorf 2015, p. 222–225.

giuliani.hönger Architekten, *Schnittwerk. Eine Ausstellung von giuliani.hönger Architekten im Architekturforum Aedes, Berlin, 22. Januar bis 4. März 2010.* Zurich 2010, p. 56–65.

Image Sources

p. 10 top: Ernst und Daniel Studer: Licht und Schatten im Pantheon, in: *Archithese* 1, 1997, p. 29

p. 8 bottom: Dan Costa Baciu / Sebastian Heeb: Die schönsten Bauten 1960–75: von Otterlo zur Ölkrise. Zürich 2013, Nr. 35

p. 12: Paolo Portoghesi: Francesco Borromini, Mailand 1990, P. 88

p. 13: Robert McCarter: Louis I Kahn. New York 2015, p. 87

p. 15 top: Romaldo Giurgola / Jaimini Metha: Louis I. Kahn. Bologna 1981, p. 151

p. 15 bottom: Hochbauamt des Kantons Zürich. Abteilung Universitätsbauten: Das Hauptgebäude der Universität Zürich von Curjel+Moser. Eine Ausstellung des Kunstgeschichtlichen Seminars der Universität Zürich. Zürich 1983, p. 101 (Foto: Weiss 1972)

p. 17: Shizutaro Urabe: F. Ll. Wright. Tokyo 1967, Nr. 15 (Foto: Yukio Futagawa)

p. 20: Rudolf Schwarz: Kirchenbau. Welt vor der Schwelle. Heidelberg 1960, p. 228 (Foto: Artur Pfau)

p. 21 top: Luigi Moretti: Strutture e sequenze di spazi, in: *Spazio* 7 (1952–1953), p. 19

p. 21 bottom: J.H. Aronson: Rome 1748. The Pianta Grande di Roma of Giambattista Nolli in Facsimile. New York 1984

p. 22 top: Galerie Maeght: Chillida. Zürich 1978, Nr. 16 (Foto: Rolf Schroeter und Fritz Hammer)

p. 22 bottom: Kosme de Barañano / Lorenzo Fernández: Montaña Tindaya. Eduardo Chillida. Spanien 1997, p. 177 (Foto: Daniel Días Font)

p. 23: Architectural Record, Juni 1977, p. 98

p. 27, p. 29 top: Giuliani Hönger

p. 29: Jacques Lucan: Oma. Rem Koolhaas, Architetture 1970–1990. Mailand 1991, p. 114

p. 31: Heinrich Helfenstein

p. 32 top: Giuliani Hönger

p. 32 second from bottom: Anna Tina Eberhard

p. 32 bottom: Hanspeter Schiess

p. 34 top: Robert McCarter: Louis I Kahn. New York 2015, p. 379 (Foto: David Finn)

p. 34 bottom: Hanspeter Schiess

p. 37: Stephen Murray: Beauvais Cathedral. Princeton 1989, Abb. 36, 122

p. 38: Josef Killer: Die Werke der Baumeister Grubenmann. Dietikon 1998, p. 127, 132

p. 40 top, Claudio Greco: Pier Luigi Nervi. Luzern 2008, p. 247

p. 40 bottom: Paolo Desideri / Pier Luigi Nervi jun. / Giuseppe Positano: Pier Luigi Nervi, Zürich 1982, p. 51

p. 41: Toyo Ito, NY 2009, p. 32, 134

p. 42: Schulamt Zürich (Hrsg.): Leutschenbach. Architektur als Lebensraum. Zürich 2011, p. 26–27, 41

p. 43: Giuliani Hönger

p. 69: ETH Zürich–gta (Hrsg.): giuliani.hönger. dreidimensional. Zürich 2006, p. 38

p. 71: Werk, Bauen+Wohnen Nr. 9, 2013, p. 12

p. 73: Werk, Bauen+Wohnen Nr. 11, 2010, p. 17

p. 75: Docu Media Schweiz (Hrsg.): 2016 Schweizer Baudokumentation. Rüschlikon 2016, B08.

Plans and images of semester projects provided by their authors.